"In his introduction to *Lucretius and the Logic of Venus*, V. B. Price takes us with him on a drive up the Pacific Coast Highway north of Santa Monica. One moment it's the twenty-first century and we are fleeing the heat and smog of Los Angeles, the next it's the year 79 before our era and we are heading from Rome down to the Bay of Naples. We are with Lucretius, who is 'in the midst of writing his vast poem on Venus and physics, atoms and their unaccountable swerving, and the mysteries of managing pleasure and pain.' In the densely loaded collection that follows, Price digs deep into his own experience in a context that embraces science and language, knowledge and feeling, anguish and memory. We are left breathless and grateful. This is a book to return to when we wonder—in these difficult times—if life is possible or worth the effort. These stunning poems convince us that the answer to both questions is yes."

—Margaret Randall,
author of Vertigo of Risk

"A reminder that pleasure and delight and wonder are worthy experiences in themselves, that curiosity and joy warrant poems as much as sorrow and grief do. I found myself nodding and smiling the way I do when listening to a brilliant song for the first time. There's power and beauty in Price's work. This—this is the book the world needs right now."

—Zach Hively,
author of Owl Poems

Lucretius and the Logic of Venus

Other works by V. B. Price

Poetry

Polishing the Mountain, or Catching Balance Just in Time: Selected Poems 2008-2020

Innocence Regained: Christmas Poems

Memoirs of the World in Ten Fragments

Rome MMI

Broken and Reset: Selected Poems 1966 to 2006

Death Self *(with paintings by Rini Price)*

Mythwaking

Chaco Trilogy

The Seven Deadly Sins

Chaco Body *(with photographs by Kirk Gittings)*

Documentaries

Semblances

The Cyclops' Garden

Nonfiction

The Orphaned Land: New Mexico's Environment Since the Manhattan Project

The University of New Mexico

Albuquerque: A City at the End of the World

Canyon Gardens: The Ancient Pueblo Landscapes of the American Southwest *(with Baker Morrow)*

Anasazi Architecture and American Design *(with Baker Morrow)*

Monsters *(with Vincent Price)*

Fiction

The Oddity

LUCRETIUS
and the LOGIC OF VENUS
poems in six books
V. B. Price

Casa Urraca Press
ABIQUIÚ

Copyright © 2023 by V. B. Price

All rights reserved.

Thank you for supporting authors and artists by buying an authorized edition of this book and respecting all copyright laws by not reproducing, scanning, or distributing any part of it in any form without permission from the author directly or via the publisher, except as permitted by fair use. You are empowering artists to keep creating, and Casa Urraca Press to keep publishing, books for readers like you who actually look at copyright pages.

This book and its components are human-authored and human-designed without the use of artificial intelligence. No part of this work may be used to train AI technologies or develop machine learning language models, or for similar purposes, without the express written permission of the publisher.

Original cover photograph by V. B. Price.
Author photographs by Magdalena Lily McCarson.
Set in Krete and Sirenne.

26   2 3 4 5 6 7

First edition

ISBN 978-1-956375-12-1

CASA URRACA PRESS

an imprint of Casa Urraca, Ltd.
casaurracapress.com

For Robin and our *petite plaisance*.

In Memoriam

Rini Price
Dr. Rick Peterson
Dr. Robert (Robin) George
Dr. Jim Chianci
Sally January Price Santschi
Reg Williams
Allan (Skip/Toadhouse) Graham
C.R. (Wombat) Lloyd
Michael Jenkinson
Lu Adler
Win Scott
Anne Seymour
Katherine Simons
Patricia Rouleau
Jacki Fuqua
Patrick Henderson
George Pearl
Sandy Greenwald

xiii	Introduction
1	Book I: *What Does It Matter?*
41	Book II: *What's Not Atomic?*
73	Book III: *More Than the Parts*
105	Book IV: *Pleasure and Survival*
135	Book V: *Laws of Physics and Civilization*
167	Book VI: *The Logic of Venus*
201	Concluding postscript
215	Acknowledgments
217	About the author

To say that life is nothing but a property of certain peculiar combinations of atoms is like saying that Shakespeare's Hamlet *is nothing but a property of a peculiar combination of letters.*

—E. F. Schumacher

Pleasure is by no means an infallible critical guide, but it is the least fallible.

—W. H. Auden

Not what we have but what we enjoy constitutes our abundance.

—Epicurus

Driving up the Pacific Coast Highway north of Santa Monica with the glint of sun on the water, fleeing the heat and smog of Los Angeles, you could almost be on a seaside road heading down to the Bay of Naples from Rome, the eternal city-to-be-escaped, on the way to Herculaneum for a summer of epicurean comforts and companionship. But you're in a rented Chevy turning onto the steep driveway that leads to the next best thing, the mesmerizing Getty Villa overlooking the coast on the edge of Malibu, a museum that's a lavish replica of one of the most luxurious compounds in late Republican Rome, the Villa of Papyri, with its library of Epicurean texts that Mount Vesuvius turned to char when it buried both Herculaneum and Pompeii in ash and lava in 79 CE. If you extend your imagination a moment, to a hundred or so years before the eruption, you could be accompanying the poet Lucretius, who's in the midst of writing his vast poem on Venus and physics, atoms and their unaccountable swerving, and the mysteries of managing pleasure and pain. He's calling it On the Nature of Things and you've been invited to join him at the Villa for a week or two of study, clean living, and sumptuous creative pleasures even though parts of the villa might still be under construction. As you step from your litter and leave the slaves to be watered, you enter the portico, see the false oculi on the ceiling full of flying blossoms in the sky, and move into the inner courtyard of the villa across an illusionistic mosaic floor that seems to be made of cubes. The pool with its bronze statues of the muses delights you and you might mull over once again the Master's formulae for happiness—the most pleasure with the least pain, and learning to enjoy everything. And if you are in a generous mood when you glimpse one of the countless slaves there, you'd see a person hobbled by the enormous pains of forced servitude attending behind the scenes to your aesthetic needs.

What a relief to have left the city with its million-plus people, its mobs of shoppers, its sewer streets, the racket and yowl of a metropolis growing too fast, its tens of thousands of firetrap wooden tenements, its criminals crucified, the relentlessness of its politics and the SPQR, its pick-pockets, bullies, slaves of refined ladies and strutting senators mingling like the smells of cooking and excrement.

The Villa of Papyri is a paradox, a garden of Epicurus far from the madding crowd that lacked any semblance of the simplicity and magnanimity that the Master offered in his own Garden in Athens, ca. 300 BCE, as a practical aid to the pleasures of inner peace. Perhaps Lucretius visited Herculaneum and relaxed at the villa many times over, his unmarked scrolls and writing tablets ready for his pen. Perhaps he strolled through the resort town paradise visiting many villas with the ocean breezes zephyring through the luscious gardens and rippling the reflecting pools. But this is all a poet's supposings. Very little is known about Lucretius except that Virgil read *On the Nature of Things* and thought him to be a great poet. We have some gossip from St. Jerome some four centuries after Lucretius's death that he committed suicide drinking a love potion, writing all his books (we only have one) while going mad, and then abandoning himself to hedonistic excess before exiting the world. Some scholars see this tidbit as a piece of early Christian anti-Epicurean propaganda. It is thought Lucretius died in 55 BCE, almost a decade after the struggles between Cicero and Catiline and eleven years before the assassination of Julius Caesar in 44 BCE. *On the Nature of Things* may have been written while Catiline was staging his revolt in the fateful year 63 BCE. And Lucretius's poem leads us to believe he was more than just familiar with the luxuries of upper-class Rome and the families who could afford rural retreats in the summer.

We know that he wrote *On the Nature of Things* for the poet Gius Memmius, who was also a Tribune of the Plebs, his patron, and an acquaintance of Catullus. It was rumored in his day that some land Memmius owned in Athens was where Epicurus's house and gardens used to stand and that Memmius had plans to build his own home on the site. Scholars have also observed that as Epicurus pre-figured atomic physics by two thousand years by building on the work of even earlier philosophers, including Democritus, Lucretius presaged evolutionary theory using a three-stage progression of the history of weapons and tools that gained in power and complexity, from hands, nails, and teeth, to stones and fire, and finally to copper, bronze, and iron. In many ways *On the Nature of Things* is the ancestral text of modern technology and the entwined energy of the materialistic determinism it espouses.

You can't read Lucretius for long before you feel the distant paradox of an Epicurean worldview in the midst of the madness of Rome. But the paradox, while familiar, is not exactly ours. That's the awkward peace you can find in the mulch of the ancient dead, those billions of souls invisible as ideas whirling and colliding and coalescing into the present so we, ourselves, emerge into being but then soon disappear to rejoin them. It's like that whenever I think of atoms, now, if I'm in a Lucretian frame of mind. The bulk of *On the Nature of Things* is a didactic exercise in the logic of atomism. Ours is a purely material world, Epicurus preached, composed of invisible stuff we are asked to believe in. And we do for a while not because of Lucretius's argument but because of the monumental common sense of Epicurus himself, who noted that "Not what we have but what we enjoy constitutes our abundance." So it's not too mad a stretch of the Epicurean mindset to think of the Great God Pan as the spawn of molecules formed as neurons carrying codes that are not to be deciphered but believed by evidence of existence in the mind, in imagination's forest, in the wild place beyond matter where matter like a breeze materializes into the divine.

Epicurean materialism leaves room for everything, even the numinous which is what is missing in modern science and contemporary materialistic philosophies. The modern absence of Epicurean openness to experience is what is turning our gorgeous planet into a leaden sphere of statistics and equations, industrial and nuclear waste, and continents of plastic debris floating through the dispirited vacuum of the material heavens that have no meaning but human use and profit.

Lucretius began his epic on the mythology of physics with a paean to Venus, mother of molecules, of chance, of substance, and of the ineffable and sublime. Epicurus might have scowled, on a bad day. Ditching metaphysics, as he did, so we'd have nothing insubstantial to be afraid of, only the stink and smashing of things made of the invisible bulk of his fancy of atoms, Epicurus didn't deny that Pan and Venus and the pantheon itself existed. They were not mere fabrications of imagination that popped full flower out of a black hole center from which all atomic buzzing froths over. He did not claim they were not real presences draped in culture and presumably made out of a divine kind of matter, which rendered them visible to the naked soul. He thought of them as one direction that the casino of the atoms tended to take, one that caused untold misery to human beings in the form of fear and guilt. So he put them off into a realm of existence that had no contact with ours. Pleasure is not a gift of grace but of wisdom and chance. It is an urge draped in logic and inference that has no test but one—the weight of pain it bears or its glorious softness of painless being.

For the modern reader, Lucretius takes us into a world of moral and imaginative speculation, one completely foreign to the puritanical hypocrisies of the materialistic spectrum of contemporary economic and political philosophy. It is startling at first to read of pleasure as a good, as, in fact, the ultimate good in a world of matter that has somehow, without the help of the theory of evolution, managed to produce creatures whose bodies are designed to register pain and pleasure as the dominant sensations of life. In the modern world, pain is treated as a medical difficulty and pleasure is seen as something shady, extravagant, dangerous, and frivolous. We value conformity wrapped around docility, passivity anchoring duty, and the principal virtue of going along and not being a bother. Anyone with the slightest excess of enjoyment or delight, even momentarily expressed, is looked upon with a diagnostic worry—is this triviality elevated above its station, the tip of the iceberg of licentiousness, does it betray a jocularity that implies unreliability, or is it "just" unacceptably responsive and emotionally feral, needing to be groomed and then perhaps weeded out?

To have one of the great philosophical schools of the ancient world announce not only that what the body and mind register is important, but that this forms the roots of morality and even of the moral life, is astonishing for those of us who live in a consumer culture driven by sexed-up commercialism that still considers sexuality as something akin to a naughty necessity that gets some people into trouble while it makes other people sexy rich. Pleasure for Epicurus, though, is not the kind of thing modern puritans might mean—license, indulgence, letting go, eating badly and expensively, vacationing into nirvana. Those are the kinds of things that cause pain, like most excess does. Epicurean pleasure is one of reason and moderation. It is based on monitoring and assessing the consequences of your own behavior. If something is momentarily pleasurable but causes pain or even just discomfort in the end, it does not qualify as the "good" of pleasure. Epicurus advises enjoyment. He teaches, I would say, a combination of amazement at the world in all its avatars, gratitude for what delights us, including our lives, and a sensible cultivation of what really brings the goodness of peaceful pleasure and calm—friendship, philosophy, and a refusal to do damage to yourself or to others, for whatever reason, altruistic or as selfish as staying clear of the things that would bring you grief. It is a morality of goodness based on the nervous system and on a view of responsibility that falls into the same camp as Emersonian self-reliance.

Lucretius and Epicurus give us a concrete proposal about what constitutes a good and pleasant life. It is a morality of consequences. Causing pain to others brings pain to yourself. Causing pain to yourself is an immoral folly, painful as the cosmic laughter that dogs foolishness wherever it goes. There is a logic to pleasure just as there is a logic to love. Pain of all kinds inhibits our ability to care for those who are the most important to us. Pain stymies the ministrations of Venus. Pleasure makes possible their full scope and power. And that is what this response to Lucretius sets out to explore.

BOOK I
WHAT DOES IT MATTER?

It flows out of mystery into mystery: There is no beginning
How could there be?—and no end—how could there be?

—ROBINSON JEFFERS

It's too easy. What does it matter
if it's all just a rollicking jumble
of invisible bumpings, absurd googols of them

all over the cosmos, and in each one of us
each moment, their infernal clicking?
Is matter really all that matters? Might as well start

burning books to make the hot chocolate.
What about meaning? How did the Logic of Venus,
or myth itself, pop out of the jamming of atoms,

or quarks for that matter? Is the universe an infinite riff?
Could be. But improv comes from genius. Is reciprocity,
compassion, metaphor, pleasure itself—are they just atomic?

What about mistakes, missing the mark, drooling vice?
This is too easy. Why must we imagine Sisyphus happy?

Venus Aphrodite,
mother of everything that is
and that is not—
matrix, mystery,
magician
as all maternal forces are,
balancing
experience
and infant bliss
in a single gesture
of exuberant joy beyond telling, please
explain to us this:
If all is matter
with nothing else,
why do atoms
in their grace
and absolute profusion
create in us
a way to "perceive"
what is not,
not only fictions
and metaphors sublime
but intuitions
of holy more,
a sensibility that is gullible,
that creates lies for itself to believe,
that conceives
the wild hope all of us have:
that consciousness cannot reside
just in the heads,
the atomic brains of creatures,

but that it pervades
what is and what is not,
that it is
in everything,
here and beyond
whatever else that is,
that the universe
thinks and knows?
If that isn't so,
why do the atoms make us think it?

The atoms have no will
though will emerges
from their randomness
in us.
Can something
come from nothing?
Did Neanderthals paint the bones
of their lost children
with red ochre
because their deepest senses
lied to them
in their grief,
pointing them to what was more
than what this life
all seemed to be:
that she whom they loved,
Aphrodite's daughter,
merely dust,

her humor, thoughts,
her angle of being
all now merely
scattered atoms in the void,
like her flesh and bones before them,
that she was
literally no more
than what we sensed,
and that intuition is
always false and fanciful, a property
of beguiling error
set upon us
to confound and flummox us, like a devil
made of atoms,
with its fearful premonitions?
How can atoms
create error?

If we think it's so
is it not
at least a thought
with a thought's
existence in the world?
Imagination is not a map to rely on
to get us to the grocers,
but that doesn't mean
it can't detect
reality;

it sees what it's made to see,
as much as touch or sight
or math might do. Is evolution
so profligate as to waste
organs of perception
on what is not?

The morality of pleasure—
is it really
a matter
of matter alone?
Ideas cause pain as much
as gorging or tripping does.
How do the quanta
smash their way
into creating
Vivaldi's imagination,
HD's poems?
How can myth, rumor, supposition,
wild hairs, ludicrous premises,
heavens and hells,
the pleasures of conversation,
music's ecstasy, how can they
just appear from tiny
units clicking and ricocheting?
How does art emerge
from neurons?
The mystery can't
be weeded out.

A simple and fearless life,
just the idea itself,
just the idea of myths
being metaphors
for the truth of us, just that
is mysterious enough.
A simple fearless life
full of the most pleasure
with the least pain
possible, preferably none.
But how
do moderns do that,
flailing in rising
pits of stuff and shit,
life itself
a monotony headline of horrors,
undertows, of political
vomit we cannot escape?
How can we
be simple and fearless
in a world of hysterias induced
for the profits of paranoia?
These fears
of the imagination,
Lucretius implies,
are to be dispelled by the logic
of atoms with which
the Gods of Paradox,
long debunked,
produce dream-like states
with such dexterity

they materialize
the phantasm of the species,
the madness of weather,
the fractal explosion of chance.
Would Lucretius warn us not
to be afraid of revelations,
scenarios, predictions, projections?
Are they really the malware of the imagination?
We choose
what to attend to.
Aphrodite
is real even if we see
she does not exist. Terror is
imagination's
autoimmune disease.
This doesn't mean
the chemicals it induces aren't real.
But Aphrodite is real in another way.
She embodies
imagination's purpose to perceive
beyond the senses,
to believe
what one knows
but cannot comprehend
in experience,
to see causes that point
to something other,
to break down the walls
of the movie house of sensation
to see more
than is there.

So what if
death is the end, your story of the atoms
is just another tale?
Mystery is more
and beyond
all hope,
all luck,
all reason, logic, conscience,
narrative and myth.
Anything
exclusive
doesn't add up,
does it?

Squirrel-dust-gray fur, the same dove-dust gray
    settling in the shade.

All our pleasures and distractions,
gardens like still lives, so still you can feel
the breeze moving off their leaves
like memories of a dark grove of shade across a
    meadow,
a darkness that held no fear on its cool brow,
shade where imagination grows
like trees behind those hallowed visions.

The world and its human
possibilities haunt us
like tales of tornadoes of nowhere
that grind up whole neighborhoods but leave
one house standing
… trucks disgorging soldiers
tramping up the alley behind your house,
passing by your back gate, no latch sound
… there but for the curse of chance…
Go, lay out a picnic in the grove!

Vague
cerebral nausea,
a dicky
unconscious,
blue
from brain to bowels,
irritable
amygdala syndrome,
grief, homesick for
the never-again.
And pleasure?
In the exercise
of wanting
another way.

Nodding off after white wine and lunch
    before the waiter in the grand museum
ah-hums you awake.

Finally, after fifty years,
my old friend and I
have no boundaries;
we say to each other
what we've only said
to ourselves before.
And now he's dead,
even him,
and we still gab on.

Being certain,
the cosmological
pleasure of that,
being certain
you have been
told what to do
when you asked
the emptiness
for help, and
the answerer said
the right way
every time
and you believed it.

As unconvincing
as that is
to everyone
you make
the mistake
of telling, even your
closest, longest
friends, you know
the answers didn't
come from you.
The words flowing
from your pen
are yours but
they did not come
from you either.
You really never
have known what
to say next—so
there was only
one thing to do:
believe what you
can't disprove and
don't understand,
believe
in the same way
the pain of the beloved
leads only to more
love and constancy
that can't be helped,
avoided or denied.
Both are the same.

They are what you do.
They are who and what
you are. You can't
help the words, you can't
help the love, anymore
than you can help being
right-handed or half
a year away
from being eighty-two.

Swiveling up into bed, bare feet finally free
    for the night, that first breeze
of the covers as you pull them up and then settle
    them back on your legs, airily down.

Reading about a life,
so different from your own,
yet so admirable, if not
persuasive, never to be
considered even a possible
mentor because of
the differences that would
have to be erased,
but still the example of her
will,
her willingness and willfulness
to do what has to be done,
her solidarity with the suffering

of the world, her clarity
to understand, oppose,
do right, even if the good
that's done is foolish,
foolish good, she shows you
where your own
discipline
and unbending is, where her
selfless matter-of-factness
is, even as it scares
the foolish good in you back
into the shadows of
desire.

Iced white wine under the mulberry,
    longing for history to have been
just
that much
kinder
and yet
cooled by the balm of kindness through
    the shade, you toast
the sky and the invisible
cause
you are not sure
is even there,
satisfied life itself has done its best for you
and you know you must never
do exploratory dentistry
with the gift of grace.

The soft lips of affectionate devotion, the passion
 that speaks only with the most ardent and
 vulnerable kiss.

History matters,
even if you don't mind it
at first.
It can become like a bruise
on a toe bone, hobbling you
insignificantly as to cause
but miserably as to effect
as when you first realize
the most important event of your life
is discounted by those you loved
the longest, discounted, overlooked,
ignored, forgotten, sweetly
denied, "oh of course, I forgot."
Did you really?
You forgot what I can never
not remember?
What happens to us slowly
warps us, like years and weight,
injury and posture
happen to our spines.
We distort, disintegrate,
reactivate, move onward
straight then bend but bend

from survival, from never
giving up on the great
storm of chance
weaving and unwinding
all around us, audacious
and exquisite
or dropping you,
like a stitch, or finally
sewing you
all up and over.

Like a sleek swoop of gulls across the waves,
    the inner chaos glides aside in the gleaming
    wake of your granddaughter's smile.

In summer twilight,
surveying the oases of herbs
in dark shadow soil, the dill forest
where ginger toms slumber in the shady
    furrows,
the fennel's thunder-black fronds,
garlic onion's flower spray,
the oregano reef and Maximillian copse,
the righteous soreness
of animal work, the sculpture of earth
works fertile with hope and seed
laid out in the gloaming

so that nothing cruel can intrude
at least before evening chill
drives us to the safe yellow light
and ember warmth of kitchen life
with the darling she of our secret woods.

The pleasure in
twilight fading on faces you adore,
the beautifully harsh peace of mind
their silhouettes cast on nostalgia.

The pleasure of getting out of bed in the morning
like a colt unwinding, straightening, bucking,
springing, testing its powers, up into the clover of
a day self-defined like you even over eighty. Coffee,
books, papers, long reading with sharp pencils, the
tools to sharpen them, and then the insight, the
first of the day, a line of Camus, let's say, "ethical
attention" and where that takes you, seeing as a
witness, aware of what you saw, what you know,
plus the hair shirt of fallibility, your own, setting
the scene for thought experiments: dark ally
government goons and some helpless skinny kid
running, running, finally escaping like a kite, and
you reading on, deeper, with more purpose, and all
because you chose
to arise.

Chewing cinnamon-stick stogies, taking notes
    in notebooks gray-edged
with your toil, the bricklayer effort to
    understand, leveling and joining
the facts, to not be naïve, to grapple with what
    our brains are most likely not
built to navigate, lured to the rocks by their
    sheer nude beauty alone.

Dreams scramble up
heaps of jumbled
jigsaw bits, shambles
of truth, of melting
fancy chocolates filled
with cortisol scabs,
amygdala carpet stains,
wall smudges right
in the line of sight
of the dignified dinner guest
who you can see
cannot disguise her disgust.
The puzzle never gives
any satisfaction.
Dream pieces go missing,
batted away by the cat,
half chewed by the dog,

what's left is adrift
on the card table you bump
into every night on the way
to relieve yourself
of dream spots on perfect
white dinner linens,
washing out with the last
drops of every leak that leave
their own telltale shameful hews
no remedy can remove.

Nothing escapes her attention,
not the smallest snail's shell,
not the petunias' dead-headed blossoms
on the log stump shrine to the beauty
    of departed things.
Everyone else had been a dampener,
a tamper-downer, a put-a-lid-on-it sour apple,
a hobble soul too bleak
for anyone else's joy not to be
a tiny thorn in the toe, a long hair in the teeth.
She didn't smile her way through life.
The waves were sometimes too big to ride,
but she sailed on that smile as much as she could,
and, in the end only the end could take her away
from her love affair, infatuation, with the mercy
    of beauty,
any beauty, the way tide pools cooled the sorest feet,
the way pelicans in rows skimmed the sea surface
full of storms and blooms of the sun.

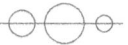

He knew when he lifted
the top of the garbage
can of the world,
the contents might be
teeming with lice.
He also knew that all
you had to do was
to put the top back on,
turn around, walk away
or just lift your head
and see the wind
in the eucalyptus leaves,
or smell the wave foam
from the sea so close
you could walk through it
and never be troubled
by hidden truths,
realities that have to be
disguised because
everything seems hidden,
beauty too.

In fact, it's often
impossible to tell
a fact from factual
fiction and fiction
from a factual lie.

It's not a matter
of being real or not.
The real world
is a story too,
more or less.
We all lie,
we all get it wrong,
but lies and mistakes
are not the same
as fiction and tales.
Lies are false.
Pleasure knows no
falsity. What we
say of it comes
from the one place
we can know directly
nothing about, except
through the flat-out
truth of the word
pleasure,
of the pleasure mind
gets from thinking
about the word,
trusting the saying
as the fact, as the key
to opening everything
one longs never
to forget the instant
after it happens
to fit the word
seamlessly as it is.

Agreeing
with being
gone,
used up, over,
dead, stone
dead, missing,
vacant, all done
and not
to be afraid
of it, then
the garden
is yours, all
yours, even if
you know you
will have to
leave it, or
that it will
desert you,
desiccate oasis,
but what
a pleasure
it is not
to waste a
moment on
tragedy, on
thinking it;
it doesn't
need your help
to be what

it is, even if
you don't mind,
don't go there.
So you don't
need to be
dutiful and
Adam-ish,
naming it,
it knows
what it is
without you.
It's not
what you
think. It's
not what
you can
know,
it knows
you, not
who
you are
but that
you are,
and were,
and that
you wanted
to stay
but zero
took you
away
and nothing
replaced
you.

The included middle.
The craftsman's
satisfaction
making books, pages
worn with handwritten
words, like soft old shirts,
ink bottles half full,
the tracks of curiosity
ever hungry, the pencil
underlines and stars
and triangles near
the planes of words
that pen-flowed
out of nothing,
including
anything that
just showed up.

The kind woman's bad joke told badly but
with intimacy and grace, and the soft,
    warm smile
of graying Aphrodite.

Newspapers rattling,
TV news gatling gun reports,
Twitter, Facebook, iPhone,
internet chaos and rumors

of confusion, and then
reality bursts though.
You in your chair reading
when a packet of notes,
the rubber bands rotted through,
falls from the top shelf
to the floor, scattering history,
letters, jottings of the moment and a list
on blue paper entitled "my experiences
of the Divine," as in "you are
your experience of the Divine."
The list was long, from prayers
answered with wisdom I hoped
to stir inside me, and elation
at the evening star, star paths
on the ocean to Chaco's code
of liberation through the trust
and pure reality of love which
can never be truthfully denied
or rationally derided. Love is
the first truth you have to face.
It makes you become who you are.
Death can too, but it's always in
second place, and way behind
love's associations, the stratigraphy
of naps, of nodding-offs, of long
deep sleeps, gentle snoozes, quick
driftings-off in the sun on the beach,
lean-backs in lawn chairs in the garden,
deep whiffling dozes in parking lots
(or as we joke and spoonerize, larking pots),
those moments of meditation where

you are and are not awake, all in
the perfect safety of being loved,
all those riches of repose,
of recharge and renewal
when the tired brain takes a break
from arduous focus and sinks
into the easy chaos of dreams,
the butter tub of reverie, not deep
but skating on the deep, warm
as a pillowed chair and closing
your eyes just to let out the sails
after a breakfast of facts
and sharp attention, just to drift
off into the pool of sun out beyond
the gentle tide.

The living heat of her hand on my arm
as she pulls herself out of bed the third time
    from the last time.

Blocks of stone, like traps
in a pharaoh's tomb
crashing down habit chutes inside us
to seal us in eternally dark and breathless
in our troubles. We don't know
what sets them sliding down,
these ten-ton blocks of thought,
but we do know they can rise.

Not that we know why or when.
We're half dead sometimes when fresh air
comes through at last, cold as a slice of light
on windy ice, though we can't escape, climb up
the chute for fear the block will crush us
sliding down again even though we see
a square of blue sky above. And then
just when hope is looking real,
the block does come crashing down again,
grinding and churning with sand
like a bottomless black solid square tornado
that just misses us. And we lean back,
pray for the strength not to doubt
too long the next time, should good luck
strike again.

A climate of depression
is a life sentence, you become
a planet brooding,
isolated by your own
eternal swirls of cloud and storm
that other people see
but cannot feel or fathom.
Climate does not come with good days
and bad, those are submerged
in the enduring pattern
that's as impossible to change,
even with supreme effort,
as the moods and prevailing
sighs of the equator.

If the world is only matter
this is what matters, heaviness
of material fate. But reality is
also what emerges
from matter, the auras
and mysteries of will,
for instance, they can't
be sensed with the atoms
of our hands and tongues,
but we know they *are*
and we know it is
a folly to deny them
as it would be absurd to deny
matter its proper realm
or to elevate it to a realm
of all or nothing, when
the "nothing" it leaves out
is so much more
that what remains
when it is gone.

Old age is orphic time,
losing what you cannot lose,
must not lose, can never lose
and all you can do
is cut your losses.
Don't lose her twice
with a backward look,
hoping to see her again
as she was. If you do,

you will lose
who she is, even if
she is no more. Do not
lose her twice.
She has become
the holy vale
of soul-making
you cannot be without.
You entrusted
your child-hearts
to each other.
You were hers.
The Valley of
the Shadow of
your Deaths
was where
you raised
each other.
It was your duty
to protect
each other's growth
without a backward
second-guessing,
without instilling
even the merest
shadow of surveillance,
alive or dead.
We gave each other
a head start—
devil take the hindmost—
and never saw
who won.

Nothing is
everything
except

everything,
and everything,
though a conception,

is impossible for us
to conceive of.
Everything does,

of course, exist.
It's just that it is
beyond the pale

of our capacities
for imagining,
or accounting. So

if everything is
unavailable to us,
we cannot rationally

or safely exclude
the possibility
of anything,

even of what's not,
especially the divine;
and though everything

includes falsehood,
reality, deceit, truth and error
we just judge what we know

by our own sense
of what is real,
our own logic that

everything is
everything.
We can conceive

of it, though
it is
inconceivable.

Fluent in
kindness, as
much as in

killing,
orcas and
wolves and

us, if we must,
we tend to our own,
can be

magnanimous,
can kill and maim
and revenge

ourselves on
each other, but
the point is

they have,
like we do,
interior lives.

As with ourselves
we experience
their behavior

but not their
experience.
Their inner

lives of feeling
have the same yin
and yang of

oxytocin and
serotonin as
we do, the wet

pathways of
grief and
devotion,

wondering and inspecting, but
does the muse
flow through them?

She must in fluencies,
though, we can't translate
or decode.

To say the universe
has no meaning,
that suffering is

without a possible
purpose, is
to imply that we,

those who need meaning
and must give reasons,
are not of this universe,

that our interiority is not
a matter of atoms,
that meaning isn't

a property of matter,
that the gods are not
as real as space dust

and the endless vacuum.
We are a part and a
property of the All.

"Not what we have
but what we enjoy
constitutes our abundance,"

Epicurus said. For gratitude
to replace fear, you must think
that gratitude is as "real" as the chemicals

of the amygdala. If you think
that part of doing anything well
is described by the art of waiting for

and catching the right wave,
you are not saying that effort is
counterproductive when effort

is all. When you say self-discipline is
about gentling the bronco not
breaking it, you don't mean to imply

that we all need to be tamed
by ourselves with a bit in our mouths
doing what our will and its conditioned

conscience demand. You mean you can
become who you want to be, even if you're
not quite yet. And you don't mean

that all such desire is loving or kind.
Lucretius and the Hubble, Jeffers
and the wild god of the world,

when you assent to them you are not
saying St. Francis and Sappho
were ancient fools.

Everything is
everything,
idea, perception,

feeling
and invention
and creation—they all

belong, no one thing
of every thing can
exclude

any, or all, other
things. That
is the logical

absurdity
of the excluding
absolutes.

Lucretius didn't
finish what
he started. He

evokes the goddess,
evokes the soul, the birth
of matter, then

sets out to prove
that matter and human
matter don't

matter much, that
the lightest touch
will get us through,

that pleasure
knows no straining,
no pain, if it only…

and then he launches
lessons in the bumping
and swerving, adhering

and coming-apart of atoms
like beach sand in constant
motion, like invisible

hurricanes eternally
in commotion, and tells us
to believe it's for the best.

Coda: What Does It Matter?

The new is never over. We don't know if it's ever better
but we do know the edge of the end and the beginning
cannot stop. Eternally onward becoming through chance
and intention is all around us and within us, roving

and yearning through the thinking maze, through all
the rest outside us, what-wasn't replacing what-is
becoming itself what-was. It all matters always:
the primal law of being is this never-otherwise

flowing of time though time which is the exact
place of what it means to be alive, to be fully living
until all you are is a *was*, a primordial backwardness,
a cosmic high, smiling at loss and death as the once-

only destiny of matter, mattering now as proof
of the always-ongoing forever of never-again.

BOOK II
What's Not Atomic?

Everything important to us, that's what—conscience,
humor, good ideas, the exquisite,
all intellectual pleasures. Matter matters

but not without the rest. Could the immaterial
exist without the material? Do new ideas emerge
from a charged atomic sponge storming in the skull?

Are we all properties of quanta? Is that what I am?
Is there a quark for thought? Isn't there more to us,
to all of us and to lizards, crows, cats, moss, ferns, clouds,

so much more that we are compelled to stop
measuring and start living in awe of what evades us,
the mystery that even "mystery" can't embrace:

awe itself?! "How amazing!" Matter matters but
if you don't mind, it doesn't matter. So, mind.

Is matter moral?
Do the stars care?
Are atoms judgmental?

How can something
specific
rise from something

differently specific?
Isn't that like something
arising out of nothing?

How can love and beauty
and compassion and hate
be properties of hydrogen,

oxygen, carbon, nitrogen,
phosphorus and calcium,
and others in traces

life cannot live without?
Metaphysics must work
through the physical.

"Things" like ideas, like feelings,
must arise from something.
Nothing can come from nothing.

Or are love and fear, the immaterial,
a potential of matter itself,
the materials, themselves,

are they particles of the Holy?
You can't breed humans to get elephants.
Like creates like? How can spirit, will

be made of atoms? Be material at all?
Perhaps the matter is not
material at all, but non-

matter in which
matter is as it seems
—miraculous.

Brilliant black red
geranium blossoms
so startingly radiant
you didn't know
blood could bloom.

The pure pleasure
in knowing that now
is your refuge, that
there will never be
a scarcity of now. Now
is never gone. It's always
moving through you.
Crisis, misery, torment,
mindless joy, euphoria can

wash this now away,
then a new now appears
and another and another
some perhaps even empty
of affliction, but always
new, always there, always
open to whatever content
comes its way. Your job
is to make sure the content
is what makes life worth
life and death—you and chance:
the sole authors of the content,
you, chance, and love, that is.
And fear?
Let it be a speck of blood
in a beautifully soft-boiled egg.

What a relief to fix
a mess you didn't cause,
see what happened, find
the tracks and clues, find
the knot, find the barely
loose twist and pry it apart,
sending it off to the vale
of vanished near misses. Such a
simple freedom—the choice
of a reasoned, safe exit
out the fire door and into
the smokeless morning.

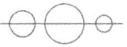

There is a peace
in understanding
that has nothing
to do with greed
for knowledge. Now
you see your life
as a puzzle
of austerity,
the very simplicity
you've admired
in yourself when you
could find it—it is
all yours in this desert
that affliction has
laid before you, this
down to the bare bones
that's becoming all
that's left, a poverty
creating a void that is
the liberation of want,
needing really
nothing more than
to use yourself
all up.

Getting her up
off the floor
where's she's made
a shiny patch
of blood, hair matted,
face red streaked.
How to get her up?
Panic dilemma and then
the solving,
the overcoming,
both such gasping,
gulping reliefs from fear,
so sweet a freedom,
like playing hooky
with no chance
of getting caught.
There she was
sprawled and now
she's standing,
moving, saying
"What happened?
No, I'm fine. What
happened. No."

Her roaring joy in the tiny cabin, snow outside,
 fingers digging into my back.

Learning, learning how
to cut the splinter
of anxiety out without
gouging a bloody hole
in my finger. No
Pyrrhic victories
in healing and cleansing,
but letting life be,
letting it have its own way,
letting the angel of happiness go
through her own kind of healing, no
trying to jimmy her
into behavior
everyone else agrees
is normal and
unremarkable, not trying
to fix her fear, fix her fatigue,
no Pyrrhic caregiving, no
pestering her into a
nagging peace of mind. Love
requires, sometimes, a hands-
off, a hands-on that has no
grab or struggle
of good intentions, just
a long whistle and rustling around
in your own life
for a while, like a lizard
learning not to make noise
moving through the leaves.

The pleasure of
making words
causes feelings
that mean
complex things.

Nothing left
to be afraid of,
nothing left
to dread,
tranquility
in the garden,
sliding into
a back booth
with your oldest
soft shirt of a pal
—*tranquilitas*,
the ultimate
of what matters,
the warm bed
of intellectual
pleasure, with
perfect covers, if
your grumpy,
worn old body
can settle down
into the soft
skin of its warmth.

The pleasure of
making your life work
for you—getting the pieces
together, seeing the patterns,
finding out how to do it—
setting ant traps that trap ants,
seeing how the tricky world,
the world of glues and gyps,
and snares and false choices,
induced dilemmas, how it
actually works, and learning how
not to be duped, how not to be
suckered and forced
to make choices between things
you don't want… if it's too good
to be true, it's probably not true,
if there are only two options,
surely they are not the only two,
if the medium is wrong
so is the message. Life is not
a scam. The IRS never
calls you up or sends emails
demanding money or jail.

The pleasure of
bamboo yellow green,
the deep dark black
green of fennel fronds,

Christmas green
of rosemary and Bowles' Mauve,
the dusty sunset red
of the bathing robin's
robin-red-breast's
breast, the brick gray
red of the dirty patio floor,
the dark bark-brown
dirt tracked on the kitchen floor
turning into tiny dove-gray
dry dunes and scattered
dust grains, the sunny
pirate lame, not quite
ancient, loving the palette
of the world, still ravenous
still adoring…

Hunting eagles. Golden
eagles landing on your
gloved hand, heavy almost
as pumas, their hooked
eyes wandering over your
body, too well mannered
to tear you apart to look
deeply—that most pleasant
space between nothing
but beauty and the jagged
bloody possibility.

The first freedom
in all its warm naked
joy: deciding to move
and moving.

Cats, dogs, the limbic systems
of all of us intermingling
through petting, purring, licking,
whiffling, wagging, cozying,
brushing up, leaning into—all that
wordless love, the eloquent
hum of contentment, the beautiful calm
of soft cool hands sliding down.
Everything just right at last,
the eggs, the bacon, the avocado, tomato,
peace being seen as the moral imperative
by someone brave enough to say so
in a war.

The pleasure in being
a half an hour after
just missing being clipped
by an eighteen-wheeler at
eighty miles per hour,
recalling other near misses
in their spotless profusion,

just for a split, laugh-happy
chip of eternity forgetting
they were lessons in problems
where I was the inevitable
conclusion.

Big ratty old chair, pillows falling out of place,
arm rests worn, their covers worn,
their covers' covers worn, books and papers
piled to the left, pens, pencils, coffee to the right,
one low, warm yellow light, the room
book-lined, love-photo'd, stacks of tasks
and in a row the daily poem books
in their multitudes.

The old friend invented
"mind field," as in
"living and dying
in a mind field." That's
our habitat. We are never
refugees from the field.
No escape, only polishing
the surface of the sea
to shine a light to nowhere.
Our worst fears are there,
red and swollen with fatigue—

forgetting the keys, leaving
the garage door open, losing
the wallet with *everything* in it,
kidnappers at the door,
assassins shooting you when you put
groceries in the trunk of your car—
they are all there, and losing *it all*
is there too, the dread of misplacing
yourself, forgetting who you are
and letting go in a blast
of terror and frustration,
you, broken down, down at the heel,
becoming a nag. Loathsome shame.
The mind field, the actual place
of our deepest sanity, our fearless peace,
the smoothness in which
the kind well of conscience
grows our salvation—
learning not to mind
in the mind field is
the greatest social peace
we can find. The strategy
is to live what we know. It's never
the darling of the world gone wrong
that explodes our horrors
in our faces; it's all on us, on us
not being wisely sensitive enough.
If you don't mind it
in the mind field,
it doesn't matter
anywhere you are.

If you don't mind,
you see foibles of others as your own
which you allow with an almost
instinctive self-satisfaction as you
defuse them. If you don't mind
there's no pain of pressure, no
gnawing of stress, no social
adrenaline avalanching panic,
no disguising our desperation as calm
trying to help someone else
end their panic, and so
no failed coercion, no resentment,
no mind field explosions
to dart and weave through
like a bad silent movie.
Not minding in the mind field
that's the wisdom of overlooking
what we've looked for mostly
in all the wrong places
all our long, wrongminded lives.

Waking up to hot sweet coffee, not
having to plan a dire escape,
blisters are pure bliss
compared to terror, and you have
no blisters yet.

Cold vegetable juice, vodka, hot sauce,
over ice, the baking heat, watering lilacs,
trumpet vine, on the lookout for toads,
for a squirrel throwing dirt on a thick, black
snake, hissing, lunging, the bunny watching
from the safety of shade five feet away.

Loneliness, pseudo-faux
widowhood, victims of luck,
of fate, of history—aren't
all of us? But does this
"all of us" make each of us
less pained? Nine billion
invisible tragedies
bind us all together
with the thinnest sutures
of grief. Koreans, Alaskans,
Argentines, Mainers, Kenyans,
Sioux, the slumlords of Hong Kong,
all of us in mortal free fall
watching the world's terror
of blowing up, of rains of fire,
of Ragnarök, Armageddon, all
battles of the end times,
all the senseless, lethal
right places at all the wrong times.

The grief in Hiroshima before
the bomb fell, all the mourning
mothers of boys
who made our mothers post
Gold Stars, yellow Stars of David.
This joy we feel sometimes,
cannot help but feel,
when the thumb screw loosens,
the depression of miasmic pain
is blown off from an afternoon
leaving us aching with old pain
but relieved if not happy,
happy if not ecstatic.
Melancholia, the steamroller,
the great leveler.
You couldn't have imagined
any of this; it's just beyond
any story or dream you've
ever told yourself—this slow
calamity of mind
and heartbreaking
sadness at the proud
sincerity of hopeless effort.
Out of the blue, as life usually is,
or always is, it just came that way
nothing really following
as in premises and conclusions.
Not random either,
not without precedent just
unforeseeable. A complexity
of personality not in theory

but evolving in the context
of the unpredictable and normal,
not scattered but not dependable.
How do you live with that?
Blind luck?
Blind faith?
By trusting
as you always have
when times were sweet
and dear, wholly good?
Learn from your responses.
You have no idea which part of you
will show up and which will need
to be pushed back or pried out,
or moved into partial shade
or just be the best of you
pathfinding through the thicket once again.

The pleasure of
closing your eyes
anytime… closing
your eyes then
counting your breaths
then starting again
and again. Ethical
attention: like breathing,
knowing what is wrong,
knowing what is right,
knowing how to say
what must be said,

as horrifying as it is,
said in such a way that
action is a definition,
that everything falls
into place, fitting
your energy like the right
combination of the lock.

She was the best. She felt like shit,
legs and back aching, memory ragged
late at night, but she was game,
so game she goes on the road
not quite clear all the time where she is
but always present, always kind, always
gentle and forgiving, always open
to a symphony of birds
in weed trees near the tracks,
malaise notwithstanding, malaise pains,
malaise fatigue, no motive power,
only her generous and endearing will,
her refusal to feel self-pity,
keeping its saturation out
by a native and self-nurturing love
of being alive, no matter the form
it's taking at the moment, no matter what,
she was loyal to love as it is.

Slipping into the soft old shirt you know
has always made you look
as good as you want to feel. Soft
old hankies, bandanas, soft
from wear and washing, washing
and wind sun on the clothesline,
comfort on the skin, her hand
on your back, your hand
on her belly, the world
as casual and thrilling
as the touch of long, old,
weathered love is the truth
that has no beginning.

And where does pleasure come in,
pleasure, Epicurus said, the only good,
absolute pleasure the absolute absence
of pain?
Is pleasure, then, a "moral principle"
not just a physical rule with physical meaning?
Not to suffer, not to cause suffering,
not to fall
into pain, not to inflict it—these have
more than atomic meaning, more
than a lucky bumping
of molecules in the right direction.

But, then, what are the laws of pleasure?
Nothing too little, nothing too much?
That requires calipers and a supernaturally
steady hand. And who knows
the optimum, anyway?
Appreciate most
the moral principle
of beauty
without comparison,
beauty without
scale or measure,
beauty as it is
without perfection,
without the notion
of what is perfect,
beauty as a gift,
a code
to a holy frame of mind?
This infuses us with veneration, to thank
from the depths, to idolize the circle stone,
the wet moss, her hands, archaic smile,
the edge at the tops of trees,
a room with an easy chair, shelves
full of books you're starving to read, or admiring
the weed's tenacity,
the silver moon
rising in a stone-still pond.

The pleasure of
finishing,
of being done,
not dribbling out
to the end, not being
stymied and giving in,
but seeing there is nothing
honest or unforced to do anymore,
nothing that doesn't
have to be scavenged for, nothing
that doesn't require
a deep hole to find,
just maybe. And so now
the project is done,
and can be added to
a bigger field
of metaphor, a small part
of a vaster grace
like ink forming words
from the point of a pen
to make a whole book,
a grace that passeth all,
effort, hard work notwithstanding.

Lohengrin and Picuris
Pueblo wood charcoal
roasting ears of corn,
smudging the garden,
protecting the peace
of this piece of shade.

Making connections:
the orphaning effect
of divorce, the rage
at suicide, the intimate
horror of migrant
children snatched
from their mothers
to make a political point;
we all belong
to the same limbic
melancholy and grief
that disappear
like a highway mirage
with a comforting hand,
a kiss, a caress—pleasure
like this disperses pain
like stroking her hair
as you hold her would be
safe and sure
as a Saturday
morning before
it happens.

Out in the morning breezes,
tree shadows cascading through
the irises, the salvia, lobelia, petunias,
marigolds and portulaca, dove song,

lizard skitter, cold and green and blue
as pure as first light spreading
through the night without an edge
or a start, the glow of beginning
never ending, refuge
of health in the heat,
cool-sheet calm, a week of waves
in your sleep at the beach,
it is all yours if you want it.
If not,
it's gone so fast, so dark,
you'll never find the switch.

Wherever you are,
in whatever thing you do,
however you will,

weaving the bonds
of friendship
from listening

and asking
and saying,
that is the way

of the world
of peace and pleasure. Lucretius
would say, perhaps,

that like breeds like on a plane
of the deep unseen, so
be good to people and they

will respond in kind with the kind
of goodness in them that they find
to extend to you. Most pleasure

least pain—the atoms of trust
and kindness are so smooth
you want to touch them

and be touched, and leave
the jagged in you
locked away where you,

because you are kind
at heart, will let them stay
to be rounded and polished

by time and grief's
elbow grease and
indelible disappearance.

Pan plays dice
with Aphrodite
perched on his

haunches while
she, feet dangling
mercilessly, preens

in the mirror
of his gaze. He's
teaching her tricks

but she's giving him
free lessons in
how to succeed

without even trying,
as he licks his lips
at her ankles and she

turns over a die and
wins! There in
the Pines of Rome

Faunus ambles and
Pan feels the breezes
through his goaty locks.

Ah Roma, La Dolce, still
squeezing from its stones
up through the fountains

the nectar of sepia
twilight where we all
can sleep.

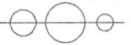

Lucretius's world
of matter without bother
of spirit or meaning,

replaces the precise
measure of pleasure
and pain for the exulted,

the blood stink
and shrieks of horror
as the body is

seared from the soul
(which atomic truth denies),
replaces its reasoned

prudence for the wild
savagery of contradiction
and the tortures of reality

we cannot bear
but must. And yet,
as we look at our pens

writing words,
look through our eyes
and hear the ink

flow lines of
thought from
the nib, we know

we are, each of us,
more than matter,
more than myth, more

and more than number,
more and more, there's no
denying it, but more

of what
and where
and why

we will
never
measure,

just as
zero is
never nothing.

Two big worlds,
the world we make
and the world wild

without us into which
we excrete our waste, deposit
our glories. The human space

polluted, despoiled, fantastic,
fabricated with the genius
of the species; everything

in my view this morning
as I write, except for my own
hands, wrists and ankles,

we have dreamed up
and made—jeans, pen,
paper, ink, watch, denim

shirt, rings, arm chair,
pillows, books, notebooks,
pencils—each formed

from something
from the world
without us,

all of it invented,
designed, manufactured,
producing waste to make,

the corpses-to-be
of obsolescence,
breakage, wearing out.

But the world without us
wears out slowly, oh so slowly,
my love, compared to us.

Coda: What's Not Atomic?

Ours is a sad world, you said, full of spasms
of tragedy and folly, a melancholy place where
a delirium of atoms comingle in exquisite, gross
appetites for becoming. We know catastrophe cancels,

comes out of the blue without even a nudge
from innocent vices. Our naughtiness, like thanks
and awareness, though, is mostly in our control,
if we learn to ride the beasts of distraction and desire.

And so we can see the merciful asymmetry of what's
in our grasp and what is not: only the gut-voiding
drops of unstoppable fate. And we are free to read them
any way that's true. A "just and pleasant" life is ours,

if we don't become monsters of the solipsistic blues
moth-holed by self-pity, too righteous to be true.

BOOK III
More Than the Parts

There's something fishy about the denial of "self,"
the final proof of "more," claiming it's just a figment.
Wet wiring brain mechanics tell us we don't exist,

that all we are is a floating network of neurological firings
in patterns that light up certain parts of the brain
on certain kinds of machines, that we are not in there,

that there's no "in" to be in, that in fact we aren't even
our thoughts, our instincts, our desires, our own creations
and inventions. There is nothing "more" to us than what

is measured. This is like saying the will is the domino effect
of a tiny, tremendous bunch of precariously piled
units, waiting to teeter. When culture is a group delusion

that fires off in different parts of different heads,
only statistics aren't fiction. What a boring story!

Our greatest pains
we cause ourselves.
They seep out
of inner conflicts,
contradictions,
of reversals that come
from trying too hard
and result in the
opposite of our desire,
our intention.
Why must this happen?
What is the mystery?
What is the machinery
of such blind misery?
It must be
that the shadow
in us is so wreathed
in terror and suspicion,
it works to contradict
everything we most
deeply want and, luckily,
most deeply fear.
The square
of black cloth
on the judge's head
means only one thing,
if you don't bring it
into the light—the judge
will know you are never
good enough
just as you are. Never,

until you give up
and turn away
from the dock
forever.

The scent of smooth, warm, tight, sun-ironed
   sheets just off the line.

Remembering everyone
who has done you good
—every friendship, every one
—the old wizard who taught you
reading was exploring, the late
lover who showed you
the delights of escaping
up the mountain to dessert
of gooseberry pie, the chum
who made you laugh so hard
at the mishaps of mistaken
identity that you broke up
at the first word of recollection
every time he mentioned it
hundreds of thunderclap,
laugh-happy times.

Death by cancer, stroke,
accident, heart attack,
a tipping point of the world,
the end of what we know
and trust, the bombs,
dictator solutions,
the cruel "cleansings"
of the old, the infirm,
the warehoused, the
symbolically different,
war in its constant
nightmare truth—forget them all,
focus on the goldfinch,
the one with the fat belly,
and scrawny one who wins
just enough
to fly, focus on
her last photograph
smiling
everything
is fine, focus
on making a good list
and following it solemnly
checking each item off
not with pride but with
relief, and focus
on the last
morsel, the abundance
of what went before it
that you did not
fail to enjoy to the fullest.

St. Epicurus, St. Lucretius,
is this your way?
The magic carpet
of extravagant now?

The world
will scathe you.
There's no way out.
You, though, must
never scathe yourself
with worry, with
chronic fear,
with paranoia.
But you will.
There's no escaping it
except
by knowing it and
practicing, practicing
not to be
the weevil of your own
misery, your own
dumbbell
torturer,
practicing to look
the other way,
not mind
and focus
on everything
else with a keenness

you reserve for
the hysterical,
exceptional,
eternal, and
the aberrant
with a beauty
you must not possess.

Fat robins
splashing
almost gurgling
in the bird bath
almost Sinatra
crooning
"Blue Moon."

Don't start fights
but look for them
and don't avoid them.
So you get knocked down,
so someone is rude to you,
insulting and threatening.
What can they do
if you are not looking
over your shoulder
trying to stay clear
of trouble? It's not

that you're cocked
for confrontation. It's
just that you know
our own inner life,
invisible to all, is all
that matters, your
calm, your humor,
your sense of play,
your own garden,
the joy of fearlessness,
the ecstasy of letting
go all restraint, all
inhibition, all conscience
for an instant you,
exactly as you feel,
with no regard
for the fist moving
at your nose
with an ecstasy
of its own, or your
facing it and
going for the
relish of the kill
and just
in time
pulling up
in full possession
of your mortal
will in service
of your common
work-a-day soul.

Trust you don't know,
won't know, can't know.
Trust there *is* something
to be known, though,
of the Divine. It is,
after all, a word
that describes something,
that describes the shadow
of something, the cracked twig
left behind by something.
Know
that you
cannot
know.
Rest in that,
trust in that.
So much pain
comes from
trying to smash,
to squeeze what
you do know
into the toy mold
of what you want
more than the truth
of not knowing.

Worrying, the festering,
then just
moving to get it
and missing it,
missing and then
feeling it, plucking it,
the thin silvery thorn
from your heel, gone as if
it had never
been there at all.

Being whole implies
that the meeting you had
with your shadow
did not
drench you
in a swarm
of ten thousand stings,
that the good
spirit in you
was strong enough
to carry
the sick child in you
to safety,
to chip him loose
like a fossil
from the inner
stratigraphy
of your maturity,

to take it to a place
you could hear it,
without letting it
replace you
with its crystal terrors
while keeping the perfect
form of who you used to be,
you, now,
listening,
remembering,
owning,
turning parasite
into companion.
That joining
will lead those
it has healed
and made whole
never to pass judgement,
knowing the hypocrite
is a self-doomed buffoon.
Know thyself means
to forgive everyone
for being who they are,
every one,
every single one,
you included.

Pan-fried, olive-oil-golden sourdough toast,
almond butter and marmalade, red fruit smoothies,
the funny papers, hot sugared coffee, cascades
of shade out the kitchen window, her impish
pleasure in being pleased.

There's profit in pain,
other people's profit
in your pain, your worry
which profiteers induce
by their "what ifs,"
prognoses, tests and
"preventions" so
they can treat
profitably
what they can't cure.
Early detection
of ills that could well
go away by themselves
if the "do something,
anything" magnates
hadn't found them out
and treated them.
Don't, the sage advises,
report your pains and worries
unless they comport
with your own commonsense,
not your larder of induced
helpless panic. Report
your pleasure, your health,

good mood, strong frame of mind,
report them,
bore them with it, there's no
profit in feeling good,
none in simply
disappearing
and then arriving
after everyone's left.

The diary, the red "words I don't know" book,
the daily poem notes, falling back
into that chair to begin the morning,
to read and work, it's falling back
into an amniotic pond without a splash,
trusting, both liberation and resistance,
starting to be who you are again reborn
every morning. The rebirths of the old
are coming back, starting over,
returning, renewed to begin afresh
on what you had left behind.
The first birth, coming in blind,
waking up and waking up again
for decades until morning becomes
Eden with temptations savored
and forgiven after all, exactly
as you've come to forgive.

The pleasure of
loving give and take,
altruism with nothing in return:
the aura of a molten core
like the earth's crust is,
a core of indefinable,
unexplainable
love that emerged
as the sum that is
more than both of us
just together,
within us
for each other
creating trust,
generative
as the logic of Venus:
like creates like,
never identical,
just as opposites
attracting are
more alike than not,
so is the work of love
so unlike effort,
but not without
striving to flow
free as exchange
with nothing to gain,
but nothing to gain
having it all,
being it all already
as two.

The heels
of her delicate white feet
in the palms
of my hands
as I leverage her
back
into bed.

Waking up to a day
without prison, without
torture, starvation,
terror, waking refreshed
and tired, but not
fearful of a slow motion
screaming
horror of a life.

The pleasure of doing the list:
recycling bottles, newspapers, paying bills, making
    the day poem, reading to the end of the
    chapters, organizing the week's pills in their
    daily boxes, folding the laundry, watering the
    big quince and petunias and bamboo and then
    just
being done,

everything
crossed off
... such rested ease
placing the first
task on the new
list in the service
of order, nothing sweeter
than everything
shipshape and watching it
unravel, melt, get chaotic
again in ways
you can always fix
with another list.

Seeing your way
clear to escape
an unsolvable
dilemma—a wall
of ice to scale
with bare feet,
a sheer cliff
of fire. Finding
the key to the tiny
door under the tiny
doormat, finding
the corner to lift up
and see the obstacle
was just a slip of paper
with fantastic art,

devised by the genius
of your fear.
You pry up the edge
delicately, peel it back,
and see open country,
the Wind River Mountains
in the far away,
the Overland Trail
just ahead, and you
with the chains sawed off
ready to plunge
into the new world
exactly
as it
is.

The pleasure of knowing
that no, they are not
straying into dementia,
senility. Oh, how those words
sink into tar. Try
eccentric, idiosyncratic,
reclusive, non-
conforming, perhaps
depressed, melancholic,
stalked by malaise, perhaps
in a web of PTSD.
More likely, "stranger"
might work,

maybe defiant,
perhaps just "their
own" person, possibly
estranged
from the folly of the world,
shy, feral, withdrawn, creative, ah
a genius, absent minded,
distracted, absorbed,
hyperattentive to what
no one else even knows
is there to attend to,
but not demented,
not dementia,
some insurance company's
anvil protocol,
never that cruel
imprecision.

Beauty overpowers everything.
Just get up on a windy morning
full of sun mere blocks from the sea,
a free child, wings uncocooning, spirit
no longer a larva wet and hard,
trees waving like sails, long before
the first injustice, the first accident,
the first malicious disappointment,
everything fresh, undisclosed,
the whole day ahead. Toast
with butter—crunchy, salt sweet,

ready for marmalade, safe
at breakfast before a human tide
jammers though the glass cables
jamming every thought. Her hands,
so tailored, so tough from gardens,
so soft from affection, stroking, holding,
calming, slightly gnarled knuckles,
a bent finger or two, brown spots,
but all like bark soothed lovingly
by a warm, smooth stone.

Always two thens—before
and after, both the same:
before and after
now. Now and once
exactly the same
as then.
Between death-self
then and then
long ago, a planet
of now,
a life-self now,
the "unique
sum of things,"
emerged and is
still emerging and
beginning to fade
at the far edges
into the ending
of now ongoing,

a now no longer
clothed in me
and my chances, choices,
and the history
I find myself
entangled with.
Soon enough
now will be no longer mine
and I will have crossed ahead
into the mystery of then once again,
then before and then ever after.
Will a new
now of mine
emerge again?
Right now,
the now I am,
this once only sum
adding and adding
holds me and draws me
into the albedo
of recollection:
the goose bump salty chill
of breezy twilight beaches; pancakes, butter,
maple syrup, Sartre, coffee steam; the first
comprehending
of Socrates; the long mud bath wallows
with Descartes, Kant, and Husserl until
experience itself demanded philosophy
to understand it;
seeing mother moving with her walker
through the fluorescent light behind the
    window, pushing on

in her orange slacks and sweater of the moment
for the last, the final time of all;
driving down the ranch road
through the yellow grasses on the way to a
bottomless perspective that doesn't have a
destination in the wind;
snow tufts and ice glass
on the mountain stream a week before Christmas
on the way to opening drawers of arrowheads,
silver match cases, milagros of tin and silver;
Christmas eves, the poems,
the trees of child delight; Rockwell
families tucked in snug, knee-deep
in snow pulling them, lightless through the canyon
to the truck in a howler with beans freezing
and blowing off the forks;
that first moment you saw you were not
afraid; the first time fear gripped your throat so hard
    and grim
you couldn't speak a word to the assembled until
you turned your back, put on a mask, and were
no longer you;
the ant hill of near misses still crawling around
    in your skull,
the elk that saw you first, inches from the car in front,
    a car coming at you
and you pulling back in just a second before the crash;
the moment at Chaco's rim bursting with light,
    knowing I could fall
over the edge and it wouldn't be wrong, not a cosmic
tragedy, just an *is* I wouldn't like;

that feeling of true grief and adoration, the terrible
    long fall into loss;
the dart games under the big tree shade in summer,
the green beans surging into Tarzan jungles
    up their poles, the wind's
infatuations with wild and billowing clouds,
    garlic, and she
with a blue scarf tied back around her hair, smiling
    the smile of angels
loving you in heaven.

The pleasure of knowing
who you think you are
and who others think you are
is not the same, subtly or generally,
and that you are
in charge of your own
image even when you know
that others have another.
You can't trick them into seeing you
as you see yourself, that's not it,
but you can lead them into having
an image that is the spitting image
you want them to have, if indeed
you want it, a good one that is not,
necessarily, authentic, any more than your
image of them is true to the form
of theirs of themselves. But, of course,

the adventure of identity
is far more thrilling than that
—a bank of funhouse mirrors
in the fire escape with their
infinite variety of warping
everything, even control, so called,
so you are left completely
up to your own
sense of integrity
—puzzling who
you are from a box
of mixed-up
jigsaw pieces, each
with your face
in minutely
different shadows,
such puzzling can
over-mire our life
with the futility
of perfection
or make it a far,
delicious, lost
oasis, truly safe
beyond reckoning, even
your own.

Seeing what you thought
was iron necessity was
merely a habit dissolved

instantly by the solvent
of insight and cemented
into usefulness by familiarity,
that the chains were made
of your expectation,
of your need for constancy
and your abhorrence of
the inconvenience of
even the slightest, least
meaningful change.
And then a new idea and
"puff," literally, the chains
disappear, freedom sees
something different, finds
a new crack in the sheer
rock face, just enough
for a handhold if
you squeeze your fingers
in and don't mind cutting them.
Self-improvement, whatever
that means, is like that
all the grueling way to the top
whatever and wherever
that may be. Is the contest
with gravity worth it?
You'll know when you dream
of the view as a map to get
in and out of time for good.

Your deep morning snoozes, Pinkie in your arms,
your distance from me solaced in your dreamy smile.
"It wasn't hard to love you, didn't have to try."

Petunias in the pots,
moss rose, verbena,
salvia, lobelia too,
beans in, tomatoes ready,
knees achy, brains searching
but with sparkplugs sputtering.
Depression has not yet
turned into indifference.
Good people watch over
the little old lady
who ran her car up onto a curb
to avoid a devil driver honking
and speeding the shock and awe
of rudeness all the way up her spine.
Bad people robbing us
in gray suits with terrible ties;
the carnivorous president
lecturing extreme Muslims to help
us fight extreme Muslims;
dianthus, electric red,
telling us peace reigns
in the secret garden
guarded by pyracantha
and the look of its
gray forlorn majesty.

There is no pleasure in
sleep that feels like your body
is curled up on the sharp edges
of hot cubes of stone, sharper than
you'd ever imagined
possible (beating the burglar
with a baseball bat), slipping
into you like a shiv, a dark
shameful edge of possibility,
not a wish or a plan,
or a choice, or a desire,
an unwanted thought, a razor
imbedded in a shadow,
an idea piercing your eye
like an ice bullet, hurting,
maiming, leaving no trace
as the hot cubes move under you,
slow tectonic states of mind,
and you so awake, so
endlessly awake, trying
to adapt and forget, every
effort like an argument designed
to let peace pass you by.

It is a universal ache
you must avoid at all costs,
feeling as if your life

is just a tag-a-long
behind some dominant
other, someone else's
life carting you around
not because you are a prop
or baggage but
because you don't know
how to stop them without
hurting their fingers and
stepping on their toes
and on the backs of their heels.
It's not a matter of love
or no love, it's situational,
accidental, it's a slow,
slow smother with
a soft, soft pillow
that feels almost
like a wanted caress
just before
you start kicking
for breath.

The pleasure of
knowing it's all on you
and seeing how
what has saved you
all along now
can save you again—
counteracting frenzy,

fretting, anxiety,
whirlwinds, brain's terror
drugs triggering
mind turmoils draining
synaptic chaos—the same
practice of relaxing
what is and what totally is not,
the now, giving attention,
resting in the instant,
finding repose in the exact
nanomoment after month
either that or
the cosmos crashing
in your adrenals,
making your little life
feel like the midnight before
going over the top
at first light.

Knowing what's
really going on—
seeing your self
doing what you
know you actually
must do to have
what you want to
actually happen—
not quite like learning
that a doorknob
opens a door,

not a slamming
shoulder,
but almost—
the complications
of health and strength
and wealth—the doorknob
here is keeping track
of what you really do,
just that
all but guarantees you will
do what it is you
need to do, until
of course, entropy
trips the knob
lock and you just
jimmy it open and
start all over again
installing a new one.

CODA: MORE THAN THE PARTS

We are, and some know it, tossed into life's grumbling
wild stream of luck, with no hope of guiding where
we'll land, in the sewer or the palace, in mud or love,
war or stagnation, the bee hive or the ant hill.

Why we are tossed, why life at all, why even peril
has its worth, is like a Dick and Jane book to our
inquisitive dog. And who or what does the tossing?
Is it the work of the atoms, this universal fact

of eight *billion* lives and chance tossings, eight billion histories
side by side and intermingling, eight billion dreamers,
prisoners, eaters on this hungry green orb of gravity
—can that, itself, be without meaning more, without more

meaning than the infernal clicking of atoms colliding
like infinite motes of gnats and pollen swirling in sunlight?

BOOK IV
Pleasure and Survival

Once you know no help is coming, it comes to you.
The ancients knew how to do it: survival is a mental act,
one mind over matter combusting, monks ablaze in the streets,

immovably making a point about what?—that it's within you
to be a homey paradise or an unbearable pyre of integrity?
It's too easy to say it's all about how we react day after day

through the fumes of grief and resentment, the smoke
of our self-immolation. Too easy or not, it is *always* all on us (fun,
fascination, curiosity never sated) to find a reason to keep

true to our cloudy duty to pleasure, to find, in even the pyre,
a focus that holds our attention more than pain—a memory of
a comforting hand, a delicious patch of sky, some kiss from life

that makes our atoms want to be us, yawning St. Lawrence
over red hot coals. Minding ourselves, even on fire, we matter.

A lesson of Epicurus:
Don't let the journey
wreck the joys
of the destination—arrive
in ecstatic peace. Leave
and get home in one
piece, and not so frayed
you can't think of
the happiness you gave
yourself by saying yes.
It is moderation. It is
a fine-tooth comb.
It is the broad brush
—even harried, sweet love
prevails, if you want it to
with no doubts, or the
various thwartings
of the pathetic.

Habit simplifies.
Too many choices
complicate, distract,
entangle
and make you fear
losing your mind
like you'd lose your keys.
Complications equal
terror's trapdoor. Fear
equals pain. Fear
eradicates pleasure,

suffocates it, becomes
the inner tornado
sucking you up
breathless amid
the debris of houses,
nails, stoves crashing
around you until
the vortex wobbles on
sucking up other
impregnable castles
while it sets you down
in the Oz of your life
so you can pull out
the splinters and begin
to heal in the splendor
of your illusions. Healing
from fear is not
a pleasure. It is a relief
which is in
suspension, waiting
for pain to clear
its black winds from the sky.

So much has to do
with description.
It can create
a reality that is
an illusion
that must be obeyed.

Description either
changes pain
to unbearable
anticipation or
allows us to overlook
what should be
overlooked, which is
of course a description
of one kind of wisdom.
Calling a passing pain
cancer, calling
confusing panic
dementia, calling
a difference of opinion
the error of the enemy,
and you've assembled
hells from the leftover
dross of your cowardice.
Oh please, let most of it
glide, slide right by,
skim the waves,
wings on a breeze,
easy with speed
without moving
a feather.

Minimizing panic when it starts—
you see there is a space between
you and your buzzing heart,

your frantic wild anxiety, feral
to the teeth, lightning terror
right there, with no clap, until
it deafens you—a space, you see it
and wedge your consciousness into it,
knowing what it means that you
and your panic are not the same.
The panic is
a ghostly veneer
full of chemical raging,
acid behind the eyes
grizzly-sighting horror
at her turning
and her charge.
But that's just metaphor.
She's not there. The panic
is a mystical dark habit. But if
you can fill the space
with fascination, then soon
panic will eject you
and you'll float in peace,
which is, in pleasure's eyes,
a perfect kind of freedom.

I imagine myself picnicking on a lawn,
    on an island meadow, surrounded by
dark woods from which vast assertions of rock
    dominate the image of the sky.

We are talking together, my dearest friends and I,
    about philosophy
and peace of mind. And I hear myself say,
    Happiness does, and what it does

best is relax and bask, and want nothing more
    than now. Then I speak up
again and say So much of art and knowledge are
    about peacefully waiting

for the right wave to come and knowing how
    to ride it without falling off,
without wasting its power and momentum.
    But why even bother, said my

contented pal, who'd survived death's mugging,
    bruised and forlorn
as he was. You bother because surf-riding, piano-
    playing, poem-making

is what you're doing with who you are.
    We're not conversing
and sympathizing to become over-boiled carrots
    and potatoes.

The idea is to become more of who you feel you are
    supposed to be,
who you've dreamed up to be, and you do that
    not by breaking

the colt of his liberty, his willfulness, because
    breaking wrecks, depresses, dwarfs.
Gentling is the best you've got, not the goad
    of the trainer

and your broken bones on the wheel of
    obedience. Do not become
your own master, though mastery is, of course,
    the purest joy.

Following the unfolding
of an honest thought,
not self-censoring,
watching it take form,
but not wantonly
or heedlessly saying
what sounds so good
you could hardly mean it.
Just trying to stay true
to what you trust in you,
a line of reason
that couldn't be helped,
no matter how fearsome
the imagined dread
consequence turning real
might be. Free risk
is a joy, you bet,
when the Gestapo is
all in its own mass grave.

Soft skin, the gaze
and patience of love,
the patience of loving
what you can never
reason with, love being
not beyond reason
but above and behind
reason, greater than all
its fumbling claims
of emotionless
supremacy.

Circumnavigating
pleasure is a terra
incognita—Puritans
of all religions and
ideologies and
theories of history
lost the good maps,
took pleasure away
from thought like a
barbed wire belt
under a nun's crisp
habit. Suffering rules;
dictionaries are rich
in describing it. But
the pleasure of being
alive, in misery or not,

falls just outside
the world's line
of thought. Blue
ocean-green fields
of onion tops, rippling
in the summer heat.
Fountain pens
that glide and slide
you right out
of your head and onto
the page without even
an indentation. Accelerating
up the street with the touch
of the ball of your foot.
A natural history
of pleasure, the next
Voyage of the Beagle.

The pleasure of a
flat-sided chunk of foundation cement
from Hacienda de los Bardos where lentil soup,
honey papers, poems were consumed
on the swirling pink and brown abstractions
of the '50s Formica kitchen table—no one would
    know but you…

Archipelagos of clouds, lily pad clouds,
O'Keeffe armadas, still lives piling,

pillowing, soaring always, sky ponds,
vapor masterpieces, bordered by
tree tops, architectural edges,
never a dead moment, even in cloudlessness,
the exhibition is always open. Just look
through the windshield, up through
the magnolias, strolling in the meadow.
This is how imagination makes
everything out of nothing.

The morality of pleasure
is a morality of denial
and of letting go
what causes pain,
a morality of calculation,
Epicurus implies,
figuring out the most
pleasure with the least
fear, the least anguish,
the least guilt,
the least shame,
ultimate pleasure being
the absence of the negative
all together. What is missing
in this primal formula
is the Aladdin's Cave
of sumptuous joys and tiny
appreciations, obsessions,
all pleasures without
the risk

of chance
going wrong
against you. The admiration,
say, of talent, of any
beauty, even of feral
intelligence wherever
it appears, in hawks,
in moss, in sea birds
diving, in ants toting
their burdens, in mulberries,
the small of her back,
the freedom of wind,
cool dips of smooth skin,
all the realm
of Aphrodite and love's
wisdom—generosity
of attention, interest,
presence, calling forth
the euphoria of being
smitten. Venus,
the knower, always
has shown the way.
World as lover
stretched out smooth
beneath your hand.

Verbena, lobelia, primrose, bougainvillea
swaying through the Pastoral, honeysuckle
breezes that don't miss a tree.

Kale forests,
a wind row
at the back
of the garden bed,
the tiniest
seeds planted
by an old
pair of hands
with no finesse
comparable to
kale's
sequoia grace.

Being at peace
with how life
has come to be,
knowing somehow
you will survive
what you don't relish,
you will endure
what you could not
bear to speculate
even a month ago,
you will somehow
learn to exist
within your means,
your emotional
and psychological

wherewithal
will be sufficient
to keep you going,
you will find a way to be
who you most want to be,
and that the carcass
of deprivation you have
worn inside you like
a carapace inside out
will crumble and leave you
free of the terrible itch
inside that has driven you
to be who you are
but now
is just like wearing
underwear of
burnt black toast.

This remembering:
He never lost
his smile blossoming
into an all-comforting grin;
Jim Crow, World War One, mustard
gas, trench warfare, rats,
mud, barbed wire,
lynchings at home
and worse. But with Tut,
Vally "Tut" Mason Don't Call Me By All My Names,
Jim Crow had to eat crow.

He was, unto himself, so
resilient, so full of empowering cheer,
he moved his family from Tuskegee,
Alabama, to Pasadena, California,
with little cash or back-up I'm sure,
worked along the way, and then
spent his days tending flowers and trees of doctors
and the lawn of a helpless actress
and her helpless child.
Among the greatest and best persons
the world has been blessed to know…
and the relief just to know he existed,
preoccupied, as he was, with humor
and its effects. The relief is
as great as the relief of limitations,
remembering
you can't
be concerned
with saying it all.
You only have six hundred words,
saying enough
is quite enough,
living preoccupied
with happiness,
giving what you have
of it to others, if they need it, is
quite enough, so much so
it becomes
all there is
to be done.

Rain roaring,
lightning blitzing
and the two of us
under our porch roof,
dry and safe,
the light still on,
the damp air seeping
coolly in through
the vents, like us who
slip inside, supper warm,
remembering
getting caught
on the ditch in a summer
squall before twilight,
the two of us finding
shelter in some thicket
of woody weeds, hunkered
down off the side
of the levee road, soaked,
making a dash to a neighboring
eave, standing under it,
pressed to the wall, as the rain
Niagra'd down in a
drip line not a foot from
our faces, thunder flickering
lights all over town and us,
drying off, watching our
whodunits, scooping avocados,
slicing cold chicken, drinking
a cold mountain stream of rosé.

All craziness, all messes, all little trips
and stumbles and losses, they all must be
overlooked and lost in the great sun
of love over all—as long as the island
of our affection remains our refuge,
the squalls, the tree-leveling
hurricanes, the volcanoes bursting, the sharks, all
swirl away, sparks from a fire,
as long as the island remains. And even if
it should physically vanish in a death, sink
under tides of voracious grief, it will still
be our culture, our language, our way of life
even if only one is left to remember, simply
because we have overlooked what doesn't matter
and have the deep sun of it, the deep light of it,
the deep warmth of it with no blackouts,
no eclipses, no promises—just like the cosmos
just is.

We sat in a clearing
in the great woods,
its breezes all around us.
None of it existed before us.
We planted it. Protected it. Made
the island of calm within it,
the oasis of light I write about
this morning with ink
flowing from a Parker 51
fountain pen, which would not
exist, superb and as-good-as

nature as it is in its
fabrication of perfection
without us, we who
domesticate possibility,
and often decimate
the chances for more.

On the road north though the great empty, cowboying our way into the high alone, without a horse or herd, driving a Japanese car, passing for locals, our politics hidden behind our grimy old ball caps, Roy and Dale forever; the Wind River mountains were ours and all free spirits seeking solace and courage; the Madison River flowing deep, dark blue blood of the West in our veins; the coffee shops, the beer joints, old folks anonymous in the all-or-nothing-else culture of two we adore as patriots and parents of the future; fishing off Malibu with a father in his sea captain's cap who made every day a birthday cake dreaming up stuff to cut the guilt with his adoring, unhappy son; eggs, bacon, hash browns, toast and jelly at the coffee shop counter, the first devoured meal of my first seven years, then stepping onto the sea-slick deck of the trawler sparkling and sharp with fish scales; running all but naked up the ditch, brown, fast, taut, past 45, Jungle Boy in the Desert Man, freer than a six-year-old climbing up the avocado tree.

When your days are numbered,
even if you don't know
what the number is, you find
you don't have emotions left
for despair. Despair implies
that things could be
better and that "if only"
things were different
you could make them so.
But you cannot. You can't.
Better isn't in range,
no sighting. Now, what is
must be plenty. And what
little of the sieve of optimistic will
you have left to you must
filter out the flotsam
of broken-heartedness,
the twigs and hairs of hopeless
disappointment, and savor
every wonder that remains.
Skim off the low-downs
and get back to living
as if each day was your
savoring lover, and all you want
is to give the same,
all of it exactly
more back to her.

Lighthearted, or
the other way:
if this
then that
in tar slime
panic surge,
adrenal tide.
Humor, or oh my god
if this isn't working
then what will?
OK, OK, this is how it is,
shooo away
knee-jerk neuroses,
lure all smiles and ease
or sink down
imagination's
quicksand with gobbling
eels and no Tarzan
to yank you out
as Nazis jab the muck
with bayonets
making even drowning
worse than dying.
It is always all
about dark gusto,
up to what you can choose,
to what altitude you can reach.
How amazing
that the holy flow
could have such wrinkles, eruptions,
blowbacks, such dandelions,

sweet breezes, pulsing boils, such wild
scheming torrents, such cold
comforts, such
soft smooth hands.

It's a tough circus trick,
learning to high fly
without a net—this not
minding pain by focusing
on everything else
that's working right, even
beautifully, and surely
the beautiful itself
is the greatest cure, though
no more, in physics, than a cool
hand on a hot knee inflamed
by stress and sciatic trouble.
Malfunctions must always
exist, must always be fixed.
They take attention, but
you can work to develop
your peripheral vision, keep
your glance there—the angels
make feather beds there.
Oh, *Hedone*, the majestic
spirit of pleasure and the world's
inner strength. *Algos*, the vanquishing
demon of pain, the world's
mechanical way of change

that none of us can avoid,
getting caught up in
tripping on the garden hose, falling
hard with the dust clanging
around us. *Algos*, the brilliant
demon of pain, disguised as worms,
as bullets, as not-so-sharp deadly blades,
Algos, the gears
of misery, which are
really the only way
that matter is, not malign,
just without
any interior, any
possibility of sympathy, though
the sympathetic species is
made of matter like all
else is. *Hedone* is
human matter's gift to atoms.
She never wavers. If you
court her constantly, worship
her enjoyment, look past
Algos to everything else,
looking for more,
looking the other way,
constantly wooing, but never
dishonoring
pain the messenger
of trouble to be fixed, if it can be,
but if not, pain is
not
necessary, like a key

to a door
never
not ajar.
There's no
penalty for
misplacing it.

You're old,
you're dispossessed,
that's the rule—
an immigrant
in your own place,
a refuge
from intimate time,
flattened
by the weight of hours,
everything
something else,
not what you knew,
an alien
in our own niche,
old friends
dust in sunlight,
old haunts
advertising sets,
shopkeeper friends,
comfortable stores
replaced with time
filled with what
is not legible to us,

as if we need a map
to our own garden,
everything an amnesia,
phantoms roaming
the brand
spanking new
looking for what
it displaced,
just swept up
shredded bills.
This must be
the loneliness of ghosts
hanging around,
watching
what happens
without them.

Happiness is
the truth
of our seeking.
It depends
on what we do
with what we know—
if we know
our impatience
harms everyone,
including us,
and we don't do
what we can
to stuff it,

then what we know
is merely, as they say,
book learning
which gets us
nowhere
if it stays on the shelf
out of our minds.
If we know
that giving to others
what they want
and need from us
is what we do
with friends
who love us
and want no
fakery from us—
if we don't
give them
what we know
they need
from us
in our deepest
truth,
our stinginess
will kill
like a spider
embalms
and drains
her prey
dry.

So we're older, we still
lust for our excitements
as we move in the ways we can,
sniffing out trails of least resistance,
trails we can naturally wobble along,
delight undimmed and proving to be
the last thing to rust up and go
out of alignment, eager, in fact,
always, always for more, but no longer
soldiers of amazement
directed by a master plan,
no longer beamed with joy
that sparks when it meets
an expectation, no longer
that kind of dutiful joy, but delight
let loose, untethered, free even of us
and what we thought we wanted.

The idea is to get by
with the least trouble
so you can preserve
your wits and strength
for what is important
to you and possibly
to invisible others, for what
only you can do. The rest
is anonymous clutter
and necessary. It must
get done, the elm must
be trimmed to suit

the neighbor, the bills
can't be ignored, the supper
must be prepared. Do them
with no friction because
the poems must be made,
books must be written,
the thoughts must be thought
and life must be adored
enough not to get in the way.

Mad men's war
looming like a hat
poised to fall from
a hat tree, bouncing
as you walk past
on the gimpy floor
boards, or the beloved
taking the rest cure
no one quite understands
but fears is a decline
when it might just be
a healing, or reading of
your father's last days
when you were there
and didn't see what
the author saw,
the Parkinson's, depression,
the will to joy,
the pleasure principle refusing
to be put on the shelf

much less die off
before the body dies
—there's a pleasure
in finding even
what you didn't know
you'd lost.

Coda: Pleasure and Survival

Eradicate illusion, we are told. The simplest is
the truest. Reduction's rusty razor. Boil it all down
to chance and the unmentioned inexplicable
and go about your pleasant life from which the miracle

of justice is said to spring, if you can walk on water
across imagination's northern sea. But you can't.
You have to dream up a different route. Without a guide,
the burden of loneliness is too much for the "pest" of self

driving you on. You need to glide on imagination
without the guillotine of true and false. Pleasure, the gift
of the "painless one," is no more an illusion than waking
to find a nightmare of cruelty has vanished once again.

Eradicate the illusion that nothing, if you will, but matter
matters. Don't think as you are told. Take no one's word for it.

BOOK V
LAWS OF PHYSICS AND CIVILIZATION

We are always just on the edge
of running out of gas, veneer peeling up,
joinery warping apart. Entropy exerting

its rule. If life is an island of order
in an ocean of chaos, it can't help but use itself up
resisting devouring tides. Decrepit, senile almost

with exhaustion, the exquisite knot that is
the Gordian orbit of life must always shore up
momentum by exploring new pleasures of wisdom and restraint

to keep the life force weaving its secret perfection
of freedom with a purpose in the dark inner place
where self and civilization are each other's meaning

and where life can resupply itself merely with hope—hope
always the insight, insight always the fuel.

There is only one failsafe for us,
the historical creature who predicts the future,
the slow-suicide species, and that is
the mystery of how now is and *is* is now.
"Then" in both its aspects,
then past, then what follows,
is our psychic downfall. *Is*
is the only exit, fragile as it is.
We are not sick yet. The world is still
holding together, the water hasn't run dry,
the bombs are still in their silos,
the oceans haven't sunk New York City, L.A.,
New Orleans, Bangladesh so far,
hordes of poor and dispossessed haven't
dragged you out of your big house yet.
Is is still *your* palace of pleasures.
Even if now has turned on Aleppo,
it will turn back, and when it turns on you
if you can stand it, it will smooth out again
even if you're too wrecked to want it.

What a pleasure it is
if you know
that ideas rule
behavior, the chemistry
of emotion as much as
forces and things,
that imaginary realities,
stories of how the world works
and what it means, that formulas

and myths create life and death,
joy and depression, purpose
and resolve, then you know
that your own thoughts,
ideas, fictions, and imaginings
create reality too, both healings
and catastrophes. We know,
like we know how to walk, that
"what ifing" calamity can cause
a state of complex fear and even
terror that is close to being fatal.
All we can do
is manage our thoughts,
preserve capacity, make sure
what is is
as we've seen it,
and that
what we've seen
is not what we think
but is
as it is
to be
thought about.

We are all creatures
of our history, of our
parents, our hometowns,
and anywhere we choose
to call home. The womb
of place is always

a portal of our unique
arrival. We cannot escape that
and even the closest
of friends, even siblings,
have lives that are so
different they might as well
be separated from us
by continents. The pain comes
from the doom of desires
for recognition and validation.
Our contexts are so unknowable
and beyond even our own full knowing
that connection, not immersion,
is all that is. How can an elephant
validate an egret? Pleasure is
being exactly who you are
even under pressure,
no matter who knows, or rather
invents and conjures, anything about it.

The sanest way
to living in peace
with another person
is believing
them, not in them,
that's too much
of a burden for
anyone, but just
taking them at
their word about

how they are doing
and who they see
themselves as being
and needing and
wanting, even if it
seems at the moment
odd and even
out of character.
Here peace is
pleasure and it comes
from not imposing
your fears and
impatience upon
those you love
when they are
working to adapt
to the new inner
conditions and
altered
capabilities
they sense in you.
Let who you love the best
have you at your best,
which your kindness is
if they love you.

You didn't agree
about the surface
complexities, but you
were both offended

and disgusted by
the same atrocities,
the same kind of
stupidity and lies,
the same manipulations,
pretensions, coersions.
So you just didn't go
to the surface, the
political fracturing,
the crumpled ice flow.
You didn't take a stand
on the bobbling and
melting fragment.
You stayed where
both your integrities
felt at home and ceased
to grow apart, and ceased
not growing together.

If the world, the multiverse, is
one infinite fabric of energy waves
and mysterious implicate intentions,
then what each of us thinks
about our health, about our world,
about everything in it, including machines,
what one thinks adds new weaves
to the fabric. And just as attitude matters
so do our hopes and intentions and our own
visualizations. The universe hates hubris,

though, because it is a futile
and damaging absurdity. Thanks is
the only inner wave in the equation
of most pleasure least pain, only thanks,
as long as it is genuine and not
a formula of self-promotion.

You know,
we all know,
the bombs
are there
on their missiles,
in their subs,
the cancer
is lurking,
the arteries are old
and cracked,
the asteroid
is zooming
somewhere too,
right at us,
the drunk driver's
vector could cross
ours today.
Now is now,
what a relief.
The pleasure
of being where
and when you are.

The innocence of it,
it's the only
worthwhile
compensation
for the endlessness
of the scathing.

Want what old friends want
or have to give you. Your needs
don't belong to them, as if
they were handymen ready
to fix the cranky problem
in the attic. Disappointments
will pile up spreading depression
through the room, halitosis
from the suave, best-dressed
dreamboat leading man.
Pleasure is an appreciation
of even discomfort
and what virtues it might require
to endure it and overcome it.

Habit is the ballast
of what we mean
by simple pleasures.
Without them the brain
must waste its exquisite

deft touch on the mystery
of where you put your wallet,
your keys, or where
your socks might be.
Fear, the great
pain of the mind,
terrifies us
with forgetting
and we remain
in a panic until
our habits are
—just so—
so we have the opening
to do pleasure's will.
You just can't do that
if your life
is completely
without some
shipshape
patterns.
Without them
art drowns
not in drink
and depression,
but sloshed
in perpetual
distraction.
I've lost my shoes.
Insight just
has to wait.

Black swans, wrong
predictions, biases
that confuse dislike

with falsehoood.
Misperception,
suspicion, supposition,

presumption—all are
illusions of light, which
leave us still groping

around, thinking
we can see in the dark. Luck,
the predisposition of others,

jealousy, being offended by
being ignored, bad moods—all
these get in the way. Friends

are environments,
places we actively
like to be, choose to be,

landscapes that
make us feel at home,
though unfamiliar

and apart. So metaphor
can often be more
than actual Gatling guns

ripping us in half. For us,
thought is the only science.
How we think, what we think,

and why, our thoughts create
our way in the world, and we
feel the pain we know and the

deliciousness that comes our way
momentarily amid normal days,
normal only for their majority

and regularity, normal for
the luck in their remarkable
uneventfulness.

Ephemera shrine, irreplaceable odds and ends,
kiva societies kept theirs
thousands of years, mine and yours are
pine needles underfoot, hot
summer afternoons, fragrant with pinecones
on countryside sidewalks in the city,
mountain musk intoxicating, the ocean
a blue chill balm just out of sight.

In our windy green oasis
trees proliferate from crows
and robins dropping seeds,

pine, pear, ash, current,
the majestic oasis fed by hoses
carrying water from reservoirs,
pumped out of aquifers,
all the shaded green and red,
startling yellows, all
artificial and transient,
bought. Of course,
in all of what we do
we cannot claim to be
responsible forever.
What we make just goes
so fast without us, but it's
as real as thought, as good
ideas, as grief like amputation,
as her soft lips on yours,
real as a cosmos
we can only suppose
doesn't know who we are.

The pleasure
in just
finding out
a probable
truth—that
the rich, say,
feel victimized
by the poor,
feel their virtue,

their arete,
their excellence
in making money
is used against them
by lesser types,
subspecies *homo
taker*, they being
homo maker,
that they feel
they are being
swarmed by take-
over rats gorging
on their substance,
that this to them
is the tragedy of
democracy—that
the superior are
required to help
the inferior when
such lowlife can
do nothing
for themselves. It is
a pleasure to understand,
to understand, that's all,
such lunacy, such
cruel mania, that
it actually exists—
the economic
taxonomy of
ravenous self-pity.

The pleasure of
understanding for once
how real things really work:
putting the pen cap back
on the back of your pen
when you're writing;
not washing the cast-
iron skillet but scrubbing it up
with salt; not overwatering
the philodendron or the Ming tree;
not going into a store
that has things you can't resist;
knowing that if you really
want to be free you must want
almost nothing;
speaking your mind
and having something you
haven't heard yourself say;
not picking on yourself at last.

Fountain grass
plumes waving
in the daydreams
of Alexander
as he passes through
the adulation
of his subjects
on the way

to soak his feet
and have the dust
washed from his
face at the sacred
oasis of Siwa
So-Far-Away,
no one but a god
could march there
and no gods would
except the kind
who anoint themselves
before accident
and germs so tiny
they can't be seen
as anything but
acts of fate
lay them to waste.
Such pleasure
in not being them, in being
off in a corner
millennia later, weaving
images in discrete
tapestries that separate us
out from the grinding
whetstone of history without
its daydreams, demolitions,
royal comforters and
lukewarm soup
in the desert cold.

Seeing how the laws
of physics play out
in daily life—force,
let's say, causes an
equal and opposite
reaction, but because
of human volatility
and imperfection
results in often
imperceptible
escalations. Entropy
itself plays out in all
attempts at order—
once we know that
we don't have to waste
sadness on being surprised
that repairs, even major
reorientations, go on all
the time in an orderly life.
Like attracts like, we know,
though opposites do attract and
repel, energy is never
lost, just changed, and entropy
is a wizard not a magician.

The pleasure of
stopping yourself
cold from going

into the dark
pit of lucrative
fascinations
with what humans
can do to each other,
the macabre cruelty,
the sadism even
that some manifest
towards those they
hate, debase,
enslave—the enemy.
Not going into that
carnarium, not opening
that pit with its black
ooze of corpses
from centuries of circuses,
not satisfying idle
morbidity presented as
novelty by
the tempters of commerce,
just refusing to go there, just
turning the other cheek
for a kiss.

The pleasure of
bringing into consciousness
what you don't want
in yourself, taking it out
of the realm of fate.

Bringing into awareness
your own predicaments
of age; you see you are not
fated to be a slave
to someone else's ending,
that you, yourself, are coming
to an end and must live now
all you can before you can't
as you near the all-over.
Even if you are alone, but
you are not, you always have
the companionship of your
projects, your study, even
your pursuit of the shipshape
—these are your secret
lovers who care for you,
look after you, make sure
you court the best.

We know the world's horrors by now.
We've seen how we kill each other
in all its hideous profusion. We know.
We don't need to be educated any more.
We know how the lovely college with its
beautiful forest growing up out of the desert
tested depleted uranium ammo,
fired into targets on the other side of the mountain
and atomized into the air around the mothers
soon to have hydrocephalic babies, just like

the ones in Basra where the Brits
used depleted uranium bullets.
We know all that—the breeze was warm
as we snoozed in the car under the shady
parking lot tree and the sweep of the Rio Grande
below us. Let's educate ourselves intensely there.

It's not about forgiving or forgetting.
The master just said stay clear
of the avalanche and slime won't
get into your boots.
The monsters come to dine
on tangerine slices and avocado cubes,
sip chilled jellied consommé and leaf through
the delicate pages of fish flesh
prepared with a perfection of dill
and lemon before them. The monsters
smile, then go home and become
all the due process that their countries need,
shooting suspects in the streets with their own hands,
with their own silver-plated elephant-
ivory-handled six-shooter given them
at state occasions on trips overboard abroad
to curry the favor of a former colonel of death
who behind dark glasses chooses not to see
the blood all over his hands or hear the weeping
of the sisters, the mothers moaning.
Executioners like popsicles and Big Macs too.

We mourn loss, we grieve heartbreak, we suffer
and if it does not kill us
it helps us make ourselves seem wise to ourselves
when we want or must change, escape
intolerable mental conundrums,
bad mind breath, homesickness
that we must kill off, die to them,
make them die to us, shed them, find new life
without them, a new "who I am,"
not a return to who I was, but a rebirth of who
I have always been at my core,
becoming, once again, true
to myself
slipping out of the noose, the security of old
torturing paradoxes, to be free of them,
even if it means
free falling
into the light
of the wildness
of beginning.

Seventy-six
Christmas mornings in my life so far, this one again
with coffee, molasses cookies, a wool scarf, lap robe,
    watch cap,
a piles of books, fountain pens, sharp pencils
shored up against the cold
in a room dark except for a stick fire in the stove

and the small impossibility of a mountain
piñon, electric
with cosmic light
delighting itself from floor to ceiling,
readying me for that feeling in me
wanting to give itself again
to those I'm lucky enough to love,
seventy-six mornings
waiting in the wings
with the mothering angels
of tender sweets,
glad, and so
patiently kind
that to remember is to be
in love again with what
might be ahead,
beautiful as a cloak of stars and comets
wrapped on the warm smooth shoulders
of Venus Aphrodite
stepping from night into morning;
even when the candle
seems snuffed out
it is still a glowing spark… quick,
take that red
tissue paper edge,
catch a flame,
light it up again,
the plum pudding
is steaming, ready to flame.

The gardens, the cats!
the volunteers! Roaming old toms
beaten up from natural selection,
war weary, wounded, almost on crutches,
the fittest but not for long,
they amble into our garden,
as wild a place as cultivation will allow,
a forest of volunteer trees, catalpa, spruce,
mulberry, and four wing salt bushes, quince,
the huge silver-leaf maple
planted from a twig, the Jerusalem
artichokes, the Russian sages, Maximilians,
and the last of the outdoor boys, a warrior
roamer named Mr. Face, too cute to be dangerous to us,
too fast and afraid to die as a mouthful for the coyote,
and yet as the volunteers
dropped from the sky to become errant pines, that cat
dropped out of our lives, and became
a monument
to the vanishing that never ends.

Broken glass, greasy strips of paper
with Velveeta stains, butts of straw wrappers
wadded, and the bottle top cutting into asphalt
at a hundred ten degrees, a receipt from McDonald's
snaking in the grass, garbage can
perfume, that wadded clump
of tissue with its white wavy wings, the gum
snot stuck under the table, the straw
and plastic top rolling in almost circles

on the path through the breezes.
What makes these different from daffodils
and dandelions?

Peace setting
over the day beginning
warm in the dawn
as a back with four layers
of cotton shirts
in a house like a big cushioned chair,
layers of comfort
so impossible for some to get,
for the street people
with cardboard signs,
"help a homeless vet,"
"so embarrassed to ask for help,"
"hungry." Or the Mexican
journalists murdered "so easy" by cartel
nihilist kids and vampire bureaucrats.
Culture, like a t-shirt and denim,
and an old padded jacket
patched and rag thin, soft
as a much-washed bandana,
that's all that stands in the way
of murderers here
in the enchanted valley
picking off easy fruit,
nearsighted
melon heads
blown away

through the cotton-
washed veil
of a soft, distracted
tranquility
masked
as a football Saturday afternoon.

We all want fun.
Fun is what makes depression
skip a beat;
it leavens fatigue,
softens sorrow,
lightens grief
like a break
to tie your shoe.
It is the antidote
we cannot endure
all the time, fun too
needs its watering down,
but ice cubes will do,
no need to seriously
measure the purring.
How can we endure it
all? All this figuring
and calculating? How
can we do it?
By taking it slowly
but with relish,
not dainty sipping, not
wishing for
forever, just a little;

that will do,
even paying the bills
needs a little sugar.

Here you are
a pillar of good sense
and strength,
efficient beyond
your own imagining,
terrified of breaking down,
leaving everyone
in the lurch, the whole
enterprise
coming down, crashing
down on our heads
because I can't keep it all
straight anymore, because
I can't walk anymore,
because the world is
topsy-turvy in my head.
Then what happens?
Now I see why people
give in, move out, get an
"assisted" life and an
"assisted" place. It's
the luck of the draw,
we have to play, or
cease to be,
and all we have
is the farm to bet.

How can you just live your life out
when the world is slowly,
doggedly coming apart around you
—the seams in your jeans popping,
cement between cinderblocks
in our bank's back wall
dribbling out like termite dust,
your own brain beginning
to drool over the top ever so slightly,
the streets' Mobius warping,
your food engineered as slow poison,
weather prying apart the drywall
all over the house, your shoes
ungluing, your knuckles
filling up with tiny ants and rust,
the soft cushions of your favorite chair
draining stuffing like your car
leaking a week's worth of oil drops
an hour. How do we do it?
Survive it? Stand it?
Want nothing. Fear nothing.
Get a good broom.

The great romance with cities
is probably over for us. The affair
with Paris, with Rome, Florence,
Oxford, even Santa Fe and Las Vegas
(New Mexico of course), the long

walks hand in hand with them,
the mystical erotic charm of our gaze
upon them, our trysts with their shade
and hidden tables, far back booths,
all evaporating now, a mild rain
on hot pavement, fast, inexorable,
watching a small splash of coffee
in a parking lot move
its edge down the asphalt slope,
drying out as it goes. These cities
that enchanted us, literally as if
an urban Pan had played his pipes
as we walked through the Luxemburg Gardens
or up Canyon Road. The Great God Pan
is NOT dead, but now there's no hope for us
keeping up with his dance, though in truth
there never was, even if we thought so.
He just wore us out with our own
feral pleasure at seeking more pleasure
and never being turned away.

One day it comes to you
to ask an ur-question.
Do wind and breezes come
from trees and weeds,
bushes, hollyhocks,
all leaves? Do they make
the air move, does the air
move at all? Couldn't life be
dependent on the breath

of plants, sending movement
into the sky? Then we learn,
"No, the air moves them, not
the other way around; but
leaves do feed us oxygen,
lungs and blood don't make it."
Do humans create war, or is
war a force of nature? Is
force natural? Or are we
the sole and sufficient cause of it?
Does war overtake us or
does it come from us?
Are these all the same
sorts of questions,
or not so much?

Your volcano just went off,
frustration, anxiety, dread,
impatience, a sense of being
dross, lint on Fate's black cape,
losing your position in your
own sense of who you are,
not that you are mind-rotted,
snorting synaptic dust, it's just
that this is so much to do
that it is so hard to do right
that if you are, to a certain
degree, what you do
the circumstance makes you
into an internal chaos,

volcanic, wanting to explode,
or to hide in your projects,
your oh so elusive
misplaced projects popping up
like a missing sock
or the ring you heard hit the floor
but couldn't find for thirty years,
the ring covered in yellow, crystalline
mouse pee, rolling out when the carpenter
pryed out the old floorboard.

Coda: Laws of Physics and Civilization

The great law is this: we appear and disappear.
Everything that is, everywhere, follows that law.
Disappearance wrecks grief upon us, not unlike
the phantom limb of an amputee. And we are

dismembered, stricken for always by all that's gone
missing. Some mourn freedom, mirrored in joy that is
always the enemy of the autocrat. There's no comfort
in power, or in atoms, in whole civilizations. whole species,

disappearing piece by piece. Vanishing is the first directive
of the appeared. Yes, we are all subject to fatal laws.
Appearing and disappearing are as steadfast as
mass and energy. Our memories and our wills are given

form by sandpiles of phantom limbs, stillborn as rose buds
that won't open, phantoms of blooming with petals strewn.

BOOK VI
The Logic of Venus

Venus can always revive the slumping of purpose
until death replaces life with the nothing that it is,
the mystery gone. The quarks in the bone dust

may be spinning but life has become a mere indentation,
a track on the page where Venus used to salsa
the laws of her logic. Of course, sages misread the clues.

Venus moves and galaxies swirl, black holes are born.
What logic! Following what follows, Venus, nude
to her very soul, disrobes us, so that divinity is skin

upon skin, minds caressing, lips on lips, fingertips
pointing the way, moonlight warmed by sun touch, touching tides
with its dark side invisible as the mind disrobed of words.

Touching, it follows, is the logic of Venus, the premise, touched
to our heart of hearts, to which, of course, only She has the key.

The simple pleasure
of making a plan,
carrying it out,
having it work
as you planned.
Cruelty is
self-evident, so is
pain you can avoid,
unkindness takes no
diagnosis. Doubt
the self-mariner's
truest guide. Brushing
aside a big "No," knowing
where you are going
and finding yourself
evading the couch
dropped off the back
of a truck at sixty miles per hour
on the freeway
just ahead, lucky
enough with the minor
skill to steer lightly,
not too much, and escape
smashing up. Oh such
exultation! There it was,
you saw it, moved
around it, and no
car was coming into
the lane you moved into,
the plan intact,
the destination still
there, luck winning

the day, luck that
controls you as much
as you have no
control over it.

The permanence of form—
a three-hundred-million-year-old
brachiopod, so long extinct
its species became stone,
only its form is as immortal
as things get, its form filled up
with pyrite replacing nacre
and shell, so beautiful
it looks like sculpture
made by genius or the divine;
the conch shell so old
it's granite, or the one
filled with quartz
and other sparklers,
transformed into a tiny
geode shell made by processes
over time even we cannot mimic;
the form of our essence
filled up with the stuff
and sidetracks of experience
all our lives, replacing ourselves
with bitterness, faults, forgetting,
or wisdom, wise as our forms—
lived as fools, sports, gamblers,
scholars—will allow.

The pleasure of knowing
it's all on you and seeing how
what has saved you all along
can now save you again—
counteracting frenzy, anxiety,
inner whirlwinds of worry,
the brain's terror potions
triggering synaptic chaos
—the same practice of relaxing
into the Only Is, finding repose
in the exact instant after instant,
being and leaving, gone
and not, now and never,
always once and once only,
either that or the cosmos
itself crashing around
in your little life, a supernova
bursting through the limbic
tangles of your heart
moment after moment,
leaving you the cindered
shadow of a person welded
to a wall at Hiroshima.

The pleasure of getting
as far as Pacheco Ranch
past down the drop

from Trujillo on the way
to Tucumcari if
you didn't turn around,
alone on the loneliest
road through the emptiest
land that seemed
as empty as I was,
full of green life but
with only one bull
to see for section
after section, lonely, bored,
wondering where
all the girls have gone.
That's not me.
I'm just vacant
without your warmth,
your smile, your hand.
Out there somewhere
is an edge then down
fast into a long
horizon with no end,
a nothing going on
for as long as infinity
seems an illusion, and me
apart from toasting you
alone at dinner, I am full
of beginnings,
empty, but the empty
of the start.

When things
make some
sense—what
an astonishment!
—when you can
tame yourself
to be who you
want to be, in
your own eyes,
grokking what
makes us want
one thing
and do another:
compulsion,
habit, patterns
of self-disregard.
If you can't
behave in ways
that lead to self-
respect, are your
standards un-
accurate, un-
improbably wrong,
are you
trying to be
who you are not?
Or have you set
yourself up
to want what you
can't have
from yourself—

have you set up
a war that only
a sudden flush,
a fast warming,
a smooth
slope of skin
can fix?
Wouldn't that
be holy fun?!

The pleasure of
not missing the love
that comes your way—
the smile of her being cozy
after you've tucked her
back into bed at three A.M.
cold from an early call
of the wild, that smile alone,
just that, is the landscape
upon which to base
an entire new life,
upon which you are basing
a whole new way of life,
just that, just that.
Slim pickin's?
You bet; so thin it really
is a vale of soul making,
a vale hidden behind
a veil of ignorance

behind which a new soul
is being made, your soul,
your territory, your fate,
she is it—*amor fati*.
Now you know.

Realizing where you are
in your life, even if it
comes with the sinking
feeling of seeing yourself
detached, unmoored, adrift,
alone—at least you know
what you have to work with.
No cheating, but useful
camouflage is possible now.
See that you are
untethered from the
beloved how-it-was
that can never be again.
It is gone, and here you are
on the open sea of the future.
Both monsters and choices
everywhere, and the shape
of Chance, the perfect Goddess,
ruling over you, a Nike
almost ready to scoop you up,
but then, of course, you have to
wake up.

Taking off,
being truly
unavailable
for a while, no
umbilicus,
incognito too,
a blank
kept track of,
I suppose, by
trackers in
the sky, but still
gone, too far
away to come back
on the whim
of someone else's
frustration. It's
that sense of
momentary,
absolute
liberty, not
exile but
withdrawal,
free of all
demands but
those of
the moment and
the moment is
filled with what
you want,

filled with
being what
freedom
is—open
to anything.

New green
leaping, time
lapsing
in the garden
after rain,
their ion bath,
not city water,
but sky water,
water filtered
through the days
as clouds pounded
clean by mountains,
slaps of lightning
like the slap
of clothes on stone,
the abundance
that comes
when the world
is right with itself
and when you have joined
as best you can
to be a part of
the green multitude
of our own

garden-mind,
an oasis before
the desert crashes
tide after tide
of sand on all
you know. It is
dawn shine.
The small hours
and their terrors
will take care
of themselves
without me
and my worrying
habit of tar pit
diving, finding
out if wisdom
works in the world,
if kindness and
humor work
in the world, are
keys to social
locks forever
otherwise
jammed
without them.
Wisdom proves
it is a way
to prevail, not
vent and lose.
Change: relax,
be still—this
isn't a put-on,

a façade, a
performance as
in all the world's
a stage. It must
be true in you,
but the least
rocky road
to take is to
allow the outward
to create the
inward, that
is the tactic
of She who
never loses,
the Nike of
freedom, gray-
eyed Goddess
who knows
how to be,
how to do,
and who you are
at your best,
and the best
is all
that's worth
the best—
the great
lasting hope
of effort.

Labels are
killjoys.
They set
limits, set
protocols, set
expectations, put
whole scenarios
into play that can
spring traps, shark
jaws on the ankle.
Adam's calling
was his sin, to start
the naming, and mis-
naming, and the mis-
nomer. So don't go
around saying that
someone is losing it,
or looks sick, or is
approaching the damned
dementia, or even a
benign word like
decline, unless you
know, and you can't,
or unless it's a joke
everyone knows. Don't
go there with your
self, and never with
others, especially
those you'd do anything
to spring free
from the dungeon
of the norm.

Pains that want to be
wooed, courted, singled out,
awarded, pains like fame,
unrequited ego, or terror
of offending and being
betrayed by some sleight
of memory or inattention,
all social pains, the generic
pain of fear induced
by encountering the unknown
and not knowing what to do.
Pains like that love you,
love and crave your attention,
can't be denied unless your
love of pleasure, naughty
or refined, is greater than
the neediness of your fear.

Do you need a map?
Here's the crude coastline of the absurd:
Connecting Thucydides and Melos
with gulags and the lunatic stupidity
of noble ends justifying means of exquisite
torture, spoken of in terms similar to those
used in perfume ads, in Martha cooking
the perfect bacon, or in the hushed tones
describing the magnificence of a twenty-five-
    year-old golfer.
Go see for yourself and send along a better map.

Such a pleasure
making real
in your mind what
reality really is,
making the real
so real, illusion,
ignorance, error,
even delusion
puff away like
measly leaves,
feeble dust swirls
on the hard pan
of the desert. Why
does this feel so good?
It's not unlike
surviving a grizzly attack
by being smart enough
to flee effectively,
working on tried
and true principles
of flight from a
superior strength that
you remember even
in a panic, like
escaping the Gestapo,
or holding off imminent
financial collapse
when you know how
the world works, know
that banks take risks
only with other

people's money and
when they fail
other people's money
bails them out, knowing
such realities like
knowing how to drive,
you feel that sigh
of relief that comes
from escaping the jaws
of your predatory ignorance,
outsmarting yourself
seeming like a sheep
but with a sharp stake
in hand, once blinded
ignorance can't make you
see what it's afraid of
ever again, until a new
strangeness wanders
onto the ship and starts
eating the sailors.

The pleasure of
simply bringing
order to the flimsy
chaos of our troubles,
the small stones
in the sandal heel
of our efforts so
easy to postpone.
Our daily drift
of tasks and fogs,

of body sinks and
hormone dumps
knocking us to a
saggy doze in traffic,
just missing being a
sadness for others,
but not sad enough
yourself to be a
sorrowful nothing
to lament in a
serious way, not elegies,
dirges, just fluttering
specks of squirrel paper
doting the moist leaves
of the green, catching
them, bringing some small
order to the dirt
feels hilariously like
a triumph, a massive
overcoming just from
that tiny sense of having
kept the tides of dross
once more from seeping
under the door and
obscuring even the
daydreams of the dog.

Vetiver in the soft
hollow of her ear
dark behind the lobe.

The pleasure of the
funny, silly, hilarious—
humor fertilized by
the mischievous non
sequitur, anything
radically out of place.
I just didn't see
that one coming, the
shaggy dog with no
punchline you can
remember wanting
to remember, fumbling
for just the exact right
word and telling it
wrong, an ultimate kind
of unhappy humor—
the slapstick tragedies
of politics, never under
estimate the evil
of the common man
in a world where
there are enough
madmen to kill
six million Jews—
the shadow number—
then kill the other
three million
"undesirables"
and *their* invisible
killers. Now that would

be a museum!
The faces and names
of the killers, their jobs,
incomes, families. No
humor in that, but
a grim pleasure
in finding out
for yourself
that genocide has two
sets of numbers,
the victims and
the liquidators, everyday
folks mostly invisible
with a bottomless pit
of hate in their hearts.
Nothing funny about that
except it's silly not
to have thought about
that before. Understanding
is a pleasure, even about
something like this,
the understanding but not
what is understood.

Knowing
that the source
of most of
your troubles
is you, and that
you know how

to fix them—
step back,
worry not,
be who you are:
change: relax,
be still.
Once you know that,
choices become
automatic,
simple, no
force, no force, no
force, liberty, no
cluttering the
freedom of
confidence, of
moral confidence
about yourself,
your abhorrence
of force and its
excrement: wasting
the simple and
clear while
fussing to make
to make the world
bend to the weakness
of your needs,
no more.

Anticipating
an empty day
—just the thought
of time empty
of dread, that
vaporous gift
of freedom so
delicious you know
you don't want
too many so you
won't lose your
taste for the best
you can hope for.

Performing well
in public, knowing
you had the luck
to do your best
at that particular
moment, and that
your best was pleasing
and distracting, rather
like making a soup
everyone can't
help but praise,
and that you,
even you, like it,
but not enough
to do it again.

Matching what is
wanted with what
you've got, a pleasure
of fitting, of joinery,
of beautiful miters,
bindings, seams.
Performing in a
groove, so the moves
you make stand out
in their perfect blending,
so perfect you almost
miss them, so self-effacing
they stand out by not
being obvious just
sublime in the way
lace can be on a
white wrist.

Most all of us
have lives that are
like a history of breezes
moving through leaves.
They happened.
Some of us wrote poems, some
read charred papyrus scrolls from Herculaneum,
some tortured patriotically,
some were wispy and tough and played the viola,
others lectured, were scholars,

changed diapers, cooked supper,
some cared for the aged and tried
to play the piano, others invented
bombs that could atomize millions,
some planted trees as an act of conscience,
some washed crude oil from gulls,
some taught workers how to read,
and most did more with their lives
than they thought they could.
The breezes show us to be
a little more than nothing,
each of us, no matter how
important the things we do.
The human forest.
A junk store of stems and twigs.
But we see ourselves
as spacious views
which seem so green, so safe,
so comforting with shade
but which we know
to be quite different
from the vantage point of our
peripheral
insider recollection—a wood pile,
a failed garden, tools
stacked like sculpture,
deep islands of green, a grove,
then elms and the occult
protection of arboring cool shadows
stretching out
for the thousands of days most of us live,
if chance is our Mentor

and loads the dice.
All of this was seen and known
by a connoisseur of clouds
on a day as grim and bleak and lonely
as losing your lover to a bear
and just escaping with half your scalp,
a day made of cold gray walls slick
as slobber, a day so hard to move
even its flimsy edges won't curl up, but even then
breezes through the trees
and discrepancies between
what you know
and what you see
found their way
through the freezing solitaire
to warm a smooth far corner
of the mind where joy and fault
grow perfectly together,
a braiding of the real
and the random told to us
like perishing shimmers
woven on a wall,
our lives themselves
charred scraps
with jottings
left behind,
brittle as old leaves
snagged on grapevines
in the early spring.

And sometime in your life,
near the end,
you are called upon to be true
with friends and loves about all
that deepest
foundational life for which
there is no true or false,
no alienation, no offense,
no difference that matters
more than being true
to the territory of true affection.
And you must learn
that you are
the source
of your misconceptions,
misinterpretations,
your wasted imagining
on worry.
You have to see yourself
as a nagging pain
sometimes,
at some time in your life,
near the end,
you are called upon to be true
with friends and loves
about all that deepest
foundational life
for which there is no
true or false, no alienation,

no offense, no differences
that matter more
than being true
to the territory of affection.
Don't worry. You have to see
yourself as the goad
for the freeing
of the independence
that binds you to the concept
of perfect freedom.
It's you, for god sakes,
not what happens to you.

Mood, "mental state," emotional
"well being," depression, anxiety,
disorder, improper
decompression, the subconscious
bends squeezing, cramping the life
out of you every time you "get better,"
tying up in the backstretch, trying
too hard, angst, ennui, mind-grime,
a poor cleaning of the lenses that smears
not clears. What is the source of it,
this molecular pessimism? Drugs
can "mend" it, but only finding
your own way out can fix it, can
solve who you are. And how
do you do that when the cause
is a matter of chemistry
and history, what is happening,

what has happened, and how
you responded? This is a mad
concoction of improbabilities,
tangles of hair and thread—can
someone else, by definition frail
and troubled, actually help
someone else? Is it enough to be
a loving crutch? Yes, as long as
the other crutch is holding you up
to your own best natures.

Good-minded thinkers,
people you never heard of really,
doing strong research,
solid thinking, compassionate
observation—you live in a place
that is like that, that really has
a local life of the mind, that treats
the here of this tiny place
as if it matters as much as Paris,
Lima, or Prague, which of course
it does. Every bus stop
is the center of the universe, every
gurney, every patch to be weeded,
every place is worth all we've got
wherever the here happens to be.
Every place needs its historians,
its serious givers of focus and the curios
of facts, every place, if just to let it exist
in someone's attentive present,

each little place
needs its Bancroft, its Turner, its Berenson,
its Benjamin, its Didion, its Randall…

The pleasure of the single tile near the lamp
and the leather couch, with its two
blue and white triangles as a flat
pedestal for the polished anthracite
black hole mirror rock, the meteor
stone heavy, melted smooth, the coin
from the reign of Julian the Apostate
loyal lover of the Gods, the fifth-century
silver coin from Athens, Her profile stamped
on the front, Her owl and olives on the back,
the cavern-black shell with the silver band
around the top, the Saturn ring sandstone
with a rough globe stone in the center from Chaco,
the turquoise mountain lake in a lump of rock,
the cloisonne pin from the National Association
of Power Engineers, the perfect ball arising
like a planet from basaltic dark cloud rock,
the polished fossil sand dollar, the slab of glass
with thin skyline blue vein visible around it,
my old St. Christopher: Hermes lugging the infant
Dionysus to safety on a hidden isle, the polished
chestnut, the basket shell with its spotted weave,
all that on the tile next to where I read
at Christmastime, icons of amazement
and the wild mysteries of the world.

The litmus test of wisdom
is happiness,
the litmus test of happiness
is self-respect.

Il Duce and Carlotta
basking in bowers of sex,
the Pond of Narcissus
their private spa with aphrodisiac
perfumes corrupting the moths and wasps
diving into honeyed cups of floral carnivores
with their medals clanking as they're chomped
and gulped while Il Duce and his darling
plot the torments of millions with a Rococo flourish;
and there we are pedestrian in our garden,
the partisans not busting down our doors quite yet,
the world run by tantrum babies who could
destroy us all on a two A.M. whim,
iced rosé in our long-stem picnic glasses,
out watering our trees
and the artful wildness
of our feral oasis, so doggedly
caressed and massaged for so many
of our shadowing decades. The refuge
of right now is here in this landscape
of our moments, so fragile, deceptively
artificial, even with the wild
four wing salt bush billowing up
everywhere, artificial as everything we do
ultimately is, artificial as time,
but real as the passing

that's pulsing through us,
memories' faint tastes and smells
beyond delicious, more seductive than a banquet.

Chaco and Delphi,
Casa Rinconada and the Parthenon,
the Aegean and the high Chihuahua Desert,
the gods whose names we know,
the gods we know are nameless,
this is the stretch from Greece three thousand years ago
to Chaco nine hundred years ago, this reality
within us, the genetic yearning
for the divine. Is this the trait of the fittest,
an accident of molecules, a strange
neural wiring passing down through
the primate way that all of us are,
as normal to us as tool-making?
I feel it in me, this recognition
of mystery and my straining need
to name it. And I cannot
name it.

He spent the next five weeks
more or less all day
in a lawn chair overlooking
a meadow surrounded by a deep
forest, the meadow with rolls and dips
and glades and carpets of green sage
and wildflowers, an ocean of meadow,

swells of land rising and falling
and he watched and gazed
and lost himself over and over,
becoming not exactly the meadow
but the enchantment of the meadow,
hungry for it, hungrier each morning
hoping against hope that nothing
might come up to disturb him
from being who he had, each day,
each house, chosen to be.

Coda: The Logic of Venus

Your motive was pure: to "secure happiness" for us
"by the shortest route." Fear not: there *is* nothing
to be feared, not death, not supernatural mythic forces
who rule the world with forlorn totalitarian power.

You achieved the shortest route by inventing a way
to make your partial world, this purely material world,
into a complete world forged from the incomplete—
your story of atoms, and our own, banishing the rest

to the status of flickering shadows, unfinished, pinched off
and squealing. Banish the fear of death because "nothing"
can't be fearful, being nothing. But we know kindness is
a greater sweetness to the kind than hate is to the angry.

Venus knows dictators loathe the subversion of joy.
    Her logic of love
is the barest of all, ecstatically more than a mere absence of fear.

WHY DID LUCRETIUS BEGIN HIS POEM on physics and the philosophy of materialism with an invocation of the Goddess Venus? Is love a mere attraction, a kind of helpless gravity, or is there a holy logic to it, a divine sense to be made both in and beyond cosmic matter, a logic to not only feeling it, but to sustaining it, and meaning it? *On the Nature of Things* postulates that everything is composed of atoms moving and colliding at random beyond perception, creating the world rather like a million monkeys with a million typewriters pounding away for a million years might come up with *The Tempest* or the poems of Catullus, or the mechanism and chemistry of photosynthesis. No matter how much logic Lucretius brings to this belief, it remains in the realm of the supernatural. The atomic theory could not be proven in any way by our naked senses (it still can't) or by any technology of the last century BCE. Yet Lucretius treats it as provable reality, while the gods, even Venus, are far distant specks of truth. (So why does Lucretius evoke Venus to be his guide if She is lounging on a pile of pillows beyond the galaxies?) Epicurus is emphatic about gods. They made and started the atoms going, but they do not mess around with human doings. It is what we think of them that causes us the worst kind of pain, psychological suffering and the horror of death. As a poem of logic, then, *On the Nature of Things* devotes itself to the logic of science, while neglecting the logic of devotion and reverence, yet using meters and locutions that are as stately as sacred texts. Perhaps this omission is an accident of composition. The poem is, it seems, unfinished. Its logical summation would be to extend Epicurean atomism more deeply and descriptively into ethics and psychology. The poem does not, however, go that far. Epicurus's theory of pleasure as the ultimate good of an atomic, material world would be bolstered by an exploration of what Epicurus calls "a pleasant life," one that is impossible, he said, "without living wisely and well and justly." And he added, it is impossible "to live wisely, well and justly without living a pleasant life," a thought that Stoics, Epicurus's rivals, would find absurd because a pleasant life in this world is too rarified to desire. I am more, I admit, an Epicure than a Stoic, for all of stoicism's Taoist-like submission to what is. I believe that a healthy life is one in which you cause yourself as little pain as possible, and bring as much pleasure to yourself and others as you can in the clean way that Epicurus calls for—in moderation, friendship, and kindness, and without fear. Despite this agreement, I find Epicurean materialism to be a dismal folly and a precursor of everything that repels me in all materialistic philosophies from scientism and Marxism to capitalism. They are soulless, ludicrously certain, and without any room for alternative, or even added, reality. They are self-consuming dead-ends, much like the metaphor of the computer to describe the brain and what it can do—in an absurd attempt to tell us who we are.

It's my feeling that Lucretius, the seemingly wealthy, luxury-loving Roman Epicure, might have thought that atomism itself was a desert of meaning, one that looked better to him than stoic resignation but one that needed the logic of Venus, in all of love's beauty and magnificence, to make materialism's mechanical sterility palatable to human beings seeking the path to a good and happy life. And what might the Lucretian logic of Venus have been? Is it a paradox: Like breeds like but opposites attract? Surely, as Emerson says, "justice produces justice, and injustice injustice." So kindness and affection breed the same. Bunnies cause bunnies, dogs cause dogs. But Venus is married to Mars. Opposites do attract. How does like breed like in polar opposites? How does that play out in the Epicurean garden of peace and pleasure? Is it a musical form of logic—like-breeds-like balanced in a fugue with opposites-attract? Is it a melody of attractions that has a Bacchian precision, not unlike the abandon and grandeur of Bacchus himself? Is it the fine line between the yin and the yang, between harmony and opposition creating a harmonic conflict that produces the music of the unforgettable? Does Venus bind difference and communion in a romantic struggle, voluptuous and divinely fraught with puzzles that only love can be patient enough to solve, to the mutual satisfaction of puzzlers in transient conflict harmonizing with each other?

As Lucretius sees Her, in the 2007 A. E. Stallings translation of *On the Nature of Things*, Venus is "life-stirring," "pleasure of men and gods," who makes "all things beneath the dome / of sliding constellations teem." She throngs:

> ... the fruited earth
> and ship-freighted sea—for (you, Venus) every species
>   comes to birth
> conceived through you, and rises forth and gazes on
>   the light.
> The winds flee from you, Goddess, your arrival puts
>   to flight
> the clouds of heaven. For you the crafty earth contrives
>   sweet flowers...
> Because alone you steer the nature of things upon its
>   course.
> And nothing can arise without you on light's shining
>   shores,
> And nothing glad or lovely can be fashioned...

Later in the invocation to Venus, Lucretius begs the "Holy One" to:

> make the mad machinery of war drift off to sleep.
> For only you can favour mortal men with peace, since Mars,
> Mighty in Arms who oversees the wicked works of wars
> conquered by Love's everlasting wound, so often lies
> upon your lap, and gazing upwards, feasts his greedy eyes
> on Love, his mouth agape at you, Famed Goddess, as he tips
> back his shapely neck, his breath hovering at your lips.

Venus is both the goddess of fecundity through divine cooperation/co-habitation, and the holy lover of the wicked, ceaseless competitor, She being the only force in the cosmos that can resist His aggression and bring Him, and the world, a moment's peace. Of course, She also presides over the battles fought in Her honor and for Her favor. And it is true that those who lose at love often feel they have lost at life. But when Lucretius asked for Venus's patronage as he started to write his cosmic poem, he understood that Her love is as binding as metaphor and simile are, both gravitational agents of difference used for the common purpose of understanding one thing in the familiar terms of another.

While many a lover has felt that the innocence of love was turned by frailty or malice into a Blakean fog of joyless experience, it's also true that the logic of Venus is embodied in the goal She implants in us to endure and achieve that wiser and happier state that Blake called "innocence regained." Venus can be considered, in this context, the goddess of rebirth, through art and passion. What poet doesn't feel the flush of being "reborn" when a poem is finished as it should be? Venus oversees birth and procreation; She also sets us forth into the Vale of Soul Making in which many of us perish by our own fine-tuned inner flaws. Some of us, though, through love's grace, find ourselves having arrived at a state of "robust tranquility" that carries us through the roiling cataracts of ambition, much like Lucretius must have hoped his adoration of Venus would have granted to him. When Venus/Aphrodite is your patron, love falls for you, allows you to manage differences with your lover in the spirit of communion. She wells up in each of us as a profound and joyous trusting of the universe that only lovers know, lovers who ascent to the mysterious reality of attraction, even though the universe, and love itself, is to us rather like William James's library where his dog likes to visit and nap, warm and quiet in the dark, comprehending only what his dog-being will allow.

Epicurus was not so modest. He believed, along with earlier philosophical speculators, that he could read the book of the cosmos and make sense of its one-letter alphabet which combines with other like letters to produce somehow the infinite variety of the material universe. Lucretius apparently believed so too, with a major caveat—that the mysteries of love are not substantial, in the sense of being composed of "stuff," but rather flow through stuff, independent of it, and one could argue *a priori* to it.

Venus, thus, represents something that is "more" as in "more than the sum of" the single atomic letter in the cosmic alphabet. She falls into a category of reality that is not accounted for in the universal theory of Epicurean atomism. She is "more" than what the theory can contend with. It has no logical place for Her. She overflows it. Much like a foreign object can destroy a neatly arranged and closed totemic system, such as that of certain Pacific Islanders who had no place for the steel ax, Venus makes atomism strain for relevance as a system which embraces everything. The attempt at making "atomism" an absolute and universal theory reminds me of entomologist E. O. Wilson and his attempts to universalize population theory and the concept of evolution through natural selection and apply it to culture and personality development. In his book *On Human Nature,* Wilson proposes an overarching evolutionary view of mind and culture, calling it sociobiology. His efforts to integrate the social sciences as well as the humanities did not go well. And instead of being a universal theory, it is "provisional," as William

James put it in his short work *Psychology: The Briefer Course*, because not everything fits "naturally" into it; in fact, not much of what is important to human beings—love, freedom, creativity, morality, comfort, art, music, or religion—fits well into a merely evolutionary view of what it means to be a human being. Lucretius, I think, realized the usefulness and emptiness of atomism as well, and simply imposed his need for "more" and his desire for an understanding of the deeper mysteries of existence on the mechanistic fancy of atomic theory. What seems apparent to me, now, is that Epicurean atomism, modern physics, and sociobiology are all unsatisfactory and incomplete views of reality when forced into the mold of a universal theory. Too much of what is important hangs out, won't fit, and is extraneous to the theory, though not to reality as we live it. Where is the room for genuine revelation, innovation, true creativity making new things (including something new almost out of nothing)? How can, for instance, the big bang theory be a universal explanation if it has to bracket what came *before* the big bang? These theories have all the limitations of sectarian religious mythology or economic theory. They universalize by excluding rather than including. So too does the Epicurean "system" of atomic properties. *On the Nature of Things* is a didactic poem, but a poem nonetheless and one which fails to convince as a "scientific" treatise but still compels us to admiration and deeply convincing pleasure as a poem.

In this sense, *On the Nature of Things*, itself, models what I'd call the safest forms of pleasure, pleasures that come with very little or very manageable pain—humor and the aesthetic and intellectual pleasures of the sane. I see Epicurean values as having a similar pyramidal structure to the Neoplatonic perspective on the "good," with pure good and pure pleasure (as the ultimate good in a materialistic world) at the top, rather like the eye of providence on the back of the dollar bill. The farther away from the top, the pure essence of the good, the less good and the more painful life becomes. Pleasure as the ultimate good is judged as being perfect and pure when tainted by no pain whatsoever. So the less pain, the more pleasure. In fact, it appears that Epicurus equated qualities of pleasure with the relative absence of pain, which means existence starts inherently pleasurable at its core. When it comes to intellectual and aesthetic joy, what can be as calmly pleasurable as contemplating the intricacies of an idea, or giving attention to a shelf full of stones and shells hand-picked by someone who loves the normal eccentricities of nature and its leavings? The perfect nautilus on my table, already cut in half to reveal a flash of its mathematical reality, has a reach invisible but to the touch. It goes from the edge to the iridescent center and circles through every chamber except the very heart, so beautiful as to be absolutely holy in its perfection, vulnerable to its flaws, soaring far above them, designed over hundreds of millions of years by the genius of surviving generations, here in my house, in my imagination, for my pleasure, frail and magnificent as all pleasure is.

Phi itself is an exquisite intellectual pleasure: 1.61803. Phi has an almost mystical relationship to the spiral of the nautilus and many other spiral forms, and to the operating principles of pleasure. It takes form in what the classical world knew as the golden section, the same form, based on the same ratio of 1:1.61803, that Phidias gave to the Parthenon. When you apply that to one's emotional health—if 1 represents troubles, and 1.61803 represents a pleasant and pleasurable life—you're in fine shape all told. Reverse the ratio and you're spinning down out of control. Spirals and the golden section are also connected in an even more mysterious way, if you're not a mathematician, with something called the Fibonacci sequence, named after an eleventh-century Italian mathematician from Pisa. The sequence turns out to be the progressive curvilinear form of the spiral, and therefore connected to phi. The sequence moves from adding a number to the number at its left. So 1 – 1 – 2 – 3 – 5 – 8 – 13 – 21 and on ad infinitum. That simple act of progressive addition gives the nautilus, as it grows its shell by the squares and rectangles of ever-larger golden sections, its irresistibly gorgeous curve. Contemplating the growth of its form gives us a deeply satisfying intellectual pleasure. And so does, I have to say, the atomism of Democritus the Mocker and the heir to his physics, Epicurus.

When a reader encounters ancient authors possessed of a profound certainty about everything and is attracted by only one aspect of their enterprise, as with my reaction to Epicurus and Lucretius, the reader can fall into the sweet pursuit of trying to figure out how an author from the past can be so right about one thing and so amusingly wrong about all else—and not because of data but because of logic. Perhaps that's what Will Durant was writing about when he named Lucretius the fourth-greatest poet of all time and attributed some of his genius not only to an inheritance from Epicurus but from what Durant called "the gaiety of Democritus." The folly of certainty can lead to hilarity, another form of pure pleasure, as when one tries to construct a universe of complexity from the crudest possible premises, i.e., that everything is made of indivisible atoms falling in their infinite numbers without touching until something causes a "swerve," as Steven Greenblatt observed in his book, and atoms start to bunch up and make stuff, everything from mice to novae and sequoias, human brains to glacial fields and automobiles.

Of all the aesthetic pleasures, there's one that rises above the rest—the contemplation of the beloved. Her smile is a history of your life of delight and relief. Seeing her face when she looks upon you with the love of the angels heals all wounds of childhood fear, even those you thought were gone without a trace. Just seeing her enter a room, just feeling that warm breeze dispersing rain and homesickness, breaks like a fever breathing out the window into a cool summer morning. What could be more free of pain than her smiling at one of your knowing looks, just the slightest up turn of the lips at an old joke no one knows but the both of you? No matter how old or frail or exhausted, her smile of love, her gorgeous kindness ends all murky sorrows, all world sadness and lonely freezing, even for you who loves to be alone. Without it, you're Li Po watching sails on the horizon move away like white flakes of grief, who knew who had just departed. With it, you're Keats with a cool hand on his brow, eyes closed, walking on water while bending slowly to write his name in it just for fun. This pleasure is pure and without danger from within, an island safe from every imperfection except what washes up and then washes out to sea. When life invades, the island sinks, the smile becomes a moon path in the night, we are forced to say, "We loved the earth but could not stay." And yet when we return, the ultimate pleasure of again and again, all over again, is ours, never thinking even once of never, but of having it all and always. Such pleasure is an ideal form of what it's like to be without fear or pain, a sacred moment, a divine enchantment. That is the concrete fact of Epicurean philosophy.

We are, some say, not "hardwired" to see pleasure first because we are genetically alert to pain and its potential meanings of harm. The modern view is that pleasure, joy, delight are acquired skills. Often life helps us out to learn the lessons of emotional self-survival, even though in dark times we think it never does. In fact, such Epicurean perfections of pleasure abound in our lives if we don't let them just whisk by. Our eight-year-old son, Jody, pounding an unopened geode with a hammer on the hearth, was almost ready to give up as the hammer just bounced off again. But then with a little more urging, he hit it hard again and it cracked in half, revealing its secret cave of dazzling crystals. His eyes got huge, he gasped and sighed with awe, there was no space between him and the delight of his amazement. And it was the same for us. At that moment, everyone in the room was ignited by the phenomenon of his utter delight. Many years before, on First Mesa at Hopi in a blizzard, my late wife Rini and I were allowed into a kiva at the village of Walpi on the tip of the mesa, down into a sacred space we had thought no non-Pueblo person was ever allowed to go. But there we were in the warmth of a tiny chamber full of children and adults who were "uninitiated" into certain Hopi religious societies, and that included us. We were in a room with dancing gods that had been with the Hopi for the better part of 1500 years, participating in a religion we could not comprehend as outsiders, but lost in the sheer, exquisite pleasure of being taken back in time to a world our imaginations and our genes understood as being wholly good. We were in the kiva for more than three hours. The twentieth century didn't exist. The dancers descended a ladder into the holy space, pounding drums replacing our heartbeats, chants, rattle sounds and bells filling the space, snow coming down through the ladder opening. Only when the mysterious snake puppet was going to be revealed were we gently asked to ascend back into the blizzard. Never in my life has there been a night like that—a drama of Epicurean curiosity and the absolute ecstasy of being absorbed totally by where you want to be.

While some claimed that Epicurus and Lucretius were the precursors of economic and scientific materialism, I've concluded that Lucretius was not a strict materialist, in the sense of the crushing domination of a world of nothing but matter which bars from reality all but the measurable, that Lucretius saw something more in life than the bump and grind, cause and effect of atoms. His evocation of Venus proves it in my mind. He is a poet not a determinist. He has experienced first-hand the unfathomable novelty of his own imagination, unwilled, almost, but working because the goddess is at his side and perhaps even holding his hand now and then. What is the "cause" that has determined *On the Nature of Things*? It's not Epicurus, not the chuckling of Democritus; in fact, nothing has. *On the Nature of Things* is a result of Lucretius's trust in the processes and mysteries of the poetic imagination, the elusive workings of the creative self which either emerges from matter, is coincidental with it, or exists in a sympathetic bond with the bodymind continuum that is still only to be sensed through its "products" but seemingly never—as yet—to be explained in scientific/analytic terms, though it can be apprehended through intuition moving through the durational reality of the flux and novelty of life. All he needs to do is court the muse by being present, by the effort of discipline, and by the patient pleasures of the trusting craftsman. Lucretius is more a proto-Bergsonian than a proto-Marxist where matter is concerned. He is willing to concede the dangers and miseries caused by superstition and dogma, but he is not willing to toss the spiritual instinct, the sense of sublime humility that comes with surrendering yourself to forces within that are aroused by the will, but are more powerful than anything you can wish for or even comprehend. He understands that change moves from what has ended into a situation of complete novelty, that evolution is creative, though not driven by a master goal. He is, in a sense, a proto-pragmatist, in that he is willing to do what works, as a poet, even if it takes a goddess's pleasure to get it done. In this sense, Lucretius appeals to the modern predicament of living in a world full of information and technique but trying to find the tatters of meaning scudding around in the underbrush, elusive and too thorny to penetrate.

In the guise of a humble supplicant praising the insights of his master Epicurus, long dead, Lucretius embraces the Epicurean effort to demystify the world, to cut reality loose from the shackles of mythology, to dispel any hope for or horror of an afterlife. He does not see creative evolution moving, if you will, beyond the atoms once they have been disorganized by the wear and tear of the life that has left them inert. He leaves the universe open in his mind so he can see, if he's lucky, what turns out to be.

I COMPOSED THESE MEDITATIONS on Epicurus, Lucretius, and pleasure in an extended community composed of Margaret Randall, Barbara Byers, Rini Price, and Robin Swift. Margaret and Barbara listened to virtually every poem in this collection as it was evolving over the last seven years. The grace and vigor of their imaginations and insight, as well as their empowering enthusiasm, energized this project from start to finish. I read many of the early poems, and discussed the idea for the project itself, with my late wife, the artist and emotional explorer Rini Price, before her tragic illness took hold. These poems were completed under the spell of my miraculous good fortune in meeting and falling in love with Robin Swift and being enlivened by her wisdom, humor, vast kindness, and integrity. I owe more than I can say to my mentor, the late Katherine Simons, whose creative presence is life-expanding to this day. I've been inspired by talking about "the Lucretius" over the years with Michaela Renz-Whitmore, Jona Kottler, Logan Kottler, Dr. Marty Kantrowitz, Mary Beath, and my publisher Zach

Hively, to whom I am so deeply and happily indebted; with the late Dr. Robert (Robin) George, the classicist and translator of Greek women poets; with Richard Fox, who introduced me to Henry James's profound advice "to live all you can"; with my sister Toria Price; with Teresa Coin and the late Dr. Rick Peterson; and with John Cordova, Bill Peterson, Kristina Yu, and Lisa Robert. I have had the pleasure of visiting The Getty Villa five times, once with Margaret, Barbara, and Rini, and once with Robin. The Villa is a reproduction of the wealthy and learned world that Lucretius inhabited at the end the Republic. Its design and curation exhibit a genius for the clarity of the simple if lavish pleasures—rooted, of course, in the abomination of slavery—that embody the hedonistic aspect of the Roman version of the Epicurean ideal.

V. B. Price has been working to repair his ignorance since he came to New Mexico in 1958 at the age of eighteen. He studied anthropology and philosophy at the University of New Mexico and has been publishing poetry since 1962. He's worked continuously as a reporter and an environmental and political columnist for nearly as long. His column currently runs at mercmessenger.com. He had the great privilege of teaching at UNM's School of Architecture and Planning and in UNM's Honors College for more than three decades. He received the 2021 New Mexico Literary Arts Gratitude Award for contributions to the life of the poetry community in New Mexico and the Southwest, and he has also been elected to the Board of Directors for the Leopold Writing Program.

His father once called him "fortune's child." The vast luck of his life is embodied in his children, his grandchildren, and in the landscape of his beloveds both in the ground and still walking upon it. His good fortune blossoms in the students who have mentored him, the friends who have taught him, and in New Mexico who has mothered him.

CASA URRACA PRESS PUBLISHES creative nonfiction, poetry, photography, and other works by authors we believe in. New Mexico and the U.S. Southwest are rich in creative and literary talent, and the rest of the world deserves to experience our perspectives. So we champion books that belong in the conversation—books with the power, compassion, and variety to bring very different people closer together.

We were proudly founded in the high desert somewhere near Abiquiu, New Mexico. Our books are available through independent booksellers everywhere. You can visit us online at casaurracapress.com to browse all editions of our books and to register for workshops with our authors.

www.ingramcontent.com/pod-product-compliance
Lightning Source LLC
LaVergne TN
LVHW040615250326
834688LV00035B/572